The Identity of Zhiqing

Outside China, little is known about the process and implications of the Up to the Mountains and Down to the Countryside (UMDC) Movement, a Chinese state policy from 1967 to 1979 in which more than 16 million secondary school leavers in different cities were relocated to rural areas. The movement shaped the lives of these young people and assigned them a shared group identity: Zhiqing, or the Educated Youth.

This book provides new research on Zhiqing, who were born and brought up after the establishment of the People's Republic of China and regarded as a lost generation during the Cultural Revolution. Presenting a remembrance of their tortuous life trajectories, the book investigates their distinctive identity and self-identification. Unlike earlier historical approaches, it does this from a social psychological perspective. It is also unique in its use of first-hand materials, as individuals' memories and reflections collected by in-depth interviews are compiled and presented as Zhiqing's self-portrait. This innovative research offers an informative and profound induction of the topic and also contributes to the development of contemporary Chinese studies by laying the foundation for a specialized Zhiqing study.

Combining rich empirical research with a strong theoretical perspective, this book will be invaluable to students and scholars of Chinese history, sociology, anthropology and politics.

Weiyi Wu is a postdoctoral research fellow at Shanghai Jiao Tong University, China. Her research areas cover youth studies, focusing on intergenerational and intergroup relations, youth subcultures, identity and global cultural industries from an interdisciplinary approach.

Fan Hong is Professor of Asian Studies at Bangor University, UK. She is academic editor of *The International Journal of the History of Sport*. Her research interests are in the areas of culture, politics, gender and sport, and she has published extensively in these fields, including the books *Sport and Nationalism in China* (Routledge, 2013), and *Sport in the Middle East: Power, Politics, Ideology and Religion* (Routledge, 2014).

Routledge Contemporary China Series

For a complete list of titles in this series, please visit www.routledge.com/series/SE0768

134 **Parenting, Education and Social Mobility in Rural China**
Cultivating dragons and phoenixes
Peggy A. Kong

135 **Disability Policy in China**
Child and family experiences
Xiaoyuan Shang and Karen R. Fisher

136 **The Politics of Controlling Organized Crime in Greater China**
Sonny Shiu-Hing Lo

137 **Inside Xinjiang**
Space, place and power in China's Muslim far northwest
Edited by Anna Hayes and Michael Clarke

138 **China's Strategic Priorities**
Edited by Jonathan H. Ping and Brett McCormick

139 **China's Unruly Journalists**
How committed professionals are changing the People's Republic
Jonathan Hassid

140 **The Geopolitics of Red Oil**
Constructing the China threat through energy security
Andrew Stephen Campion

141 **China's Socialist Rule of Law Reforms Under Xi Jinping**
Edited by John Garrick and Yan Chang Bennett

142 **Economy, Emotion, and Ethics in Chinese Cinema**
Globalization on speed
David Leiwei Li

143 **Social Attitudes in Contemporary China**
Yu Chen, Wei Fang, Liqing Li, Paul Morrissey and Chen Nie

144 **Media Power in Hong Kong**
Hyper-marketized media and cultural resistance
Charles Chi-wai Cheung

145 **The Identity of Zhiqing**
The lost generation
Weiyi Wu and Fan Hong

The Identity of Zhiqing
The lost generation

Weiyi Wu and Fan Hong

LONDON AND NEW YORK

First published 2016
by Routledge
2 Park Square, Milton Park, Abingdon, Oxon OX14 4RN

and by Routledge
711 Third Avenue, New York, NY 10017, USA

First issued in paperback 2017

Routledge is an imprint of the Taylor & Francis Group, an informa business

© 2016 Weiyi Wu and Fan Hong

The right of Weiyi Wu and Fan Hong to be identified as authors of this work has been asserted by them in accordance with sections 77 and 78 of the Copyright, Designs and Patents Act 1988.

All rights reserved. No part of this book may be reprinted or reproduced or utilised in any form or by any electronic, mechanical, or other means, now known or hereafter invented, including photocopying and recording, or in any information storage or retrieval system, without permission in writing from the publishers.

Trademark notice: Product or corporate names may be trademarks or registered trademarks, and are used only for identification and explanation without intent to infringe.

British Library Cataloguing in Publication Data
A catalogue record for this book is available from the British Library

Library of Congress Cataloging in Publication Data
Names: Wu, Weiyi. | Fan, Hong, 1957-
Title: The identity of zhiqing : the lost generation / Weiyi Wu and Fan Hong.
Description: Milton Park, Abingdon, Oxon : Routledge, 2016. | Series: Routledge contemporary China series ; 145 | Includes bibliographical references and index.
Identifiers: LCCN 2015039768| ISBN 9781138933170 (hardback) | ISBN 1138933171 (hardback) | ISBN 9781315678689 (ebook) | ISBN 1315678683 (ebook)
Subjects: LCSH: China—Politics and government—1949-1976. | China—Politics and government—1976-2002. | Youth—China—History—20th century. | High school graduates—China—History—20th century. | Urban-rural migration—Political aspects—China—History—20th century. | Group identity—China—History—20th century. | Identity (Psychology)—China—History—20th century. | Social psychology—China—History—20th century. | China—History—1949-1976—Biography. | Interviews—China.
Classification: LCC DS777.75 .W82 2016 | DDC 305.2350951/09045—dc23
LC record available at http://lccn.loc.gov/2015039768

ISBN 13: 978-1-138-30254-9 (pbk)
ISBN 13: 978-1-138-93317-0 (hbk)

Typeset in Times New Roman
by Swales & Willis Ltd, Exeter, Devon, UK

Contents

List of illustrations vi
Preface vii

1 Finding the "lost generation" 1

2 Linking Zhiqing's life trajectories to social history 13

3 To the wider world: group-identity configuration I (1967–81) 39

4 Drops of water in the ocean: group-identity configuration II (1980s–present) 60

5 The identity of Zhiqing: approach and conclusion 85

References 89
Index 96

Illustrations

Figures

1.1 Structure of social identity theory   5
1.2 Consecutive procedures of identity formation   8
3.1 Processing and analysis of Zhiqing's life stories   40

Tables

2.1 Numbers of Zhiqing (1962–79)   18
2.2 Cohort, year of birth and key years in the context of the UMDC Movement   26
2.3 Average age and age range of each cohort during the Cultural Revolution (1966–76)   29
2.4 Average age and age range of each cohort during the UMDC Movement (1968–79)   29
2.5 Average age and age range of each cohort since the Reform and Open era (1979–2012)   30
4.1 Scale of the UMDC Movement (1976–79)   61
4.2 The number of Zhiqing returning to the city through various channels (1976–79)   61

Preface

The Up to the Mountains and Down to the Countryside (UMDC) Movement was implemented in China as a state policy from 1967 to 1979, during which time more than 16 million secondary school leavers in different cities relocated to rural areas. After the abrupt termination of the Movement, returned Zhiqing strived hard to establish their foothold in the city, yet most of them ended up with low-paid jobs. Since the "Reform and Open" policy, Zhiqing have been positioned as "the lost generation", a synonym that suggests the problematization of their group identity and their socially disadvantaged status. Recently, the topic has again attracted public attention as the Zhiqing generation in China's central leadership, for example President Xi Jinping and Premier Li Keqiang, came into power in 2013. Focusing on the issue of Zhiqing's social identity and re-identification, which is less analysed in the existing literature, we hope to contribute to a better knowledge of Zhiqing and the UMDC Movement by compiling and analysing the social history and individuals' life stories.

This research was greatly aided by inspiring discussions with a group of colleagues and scholars in both China and Ireland. We owe special thanks to all the Zhiqing friends who helped this research project in various ways. Most of all, we would like to thank all the interviewees. Without their trust and participation, this book would not have been possible. We dedicate this book to Zhiqing – the generation is never lost.

Weiyi Wu and Fan Hong

1 Finding the "lost generation"

1.1 Zhiqing's identity: specificities and strategies

"Zhishi qingnian" (知识青年) is a general term that can be used to address any young people who have received a certain level of education. Hence it is often translated as "educated youth". The shortened version "Zhiqing" (知青), however, has a specific meaning because of its historical origin. In contemporary Chinese history, "Zhiqing" refers to a group of urban youth who were sent to the countryside to engage in agricultural production during the "Shangshan xiaxiang yundong" (上山下乡运动 – Up to the Mountains Down to the Countryside Movement, hereinafter, the UMDC Movement) from the early 1960s to the late 1970s.[1] During this state-led movement, the boundary of the Zhiqing group was officially demarcated and Zhiqing were defined as "urban secondary school graduates who were sent to the countryside with a state provision of settlement fee after 1962 when resettlement work for Zhiqing was taken as a special work by the government" (Ding 1998b, 259). Therefore, to the English academia, Zhiqing are also known as "Sent-down Youth" (Stanley 1981) or "Rusticated Youth" (Cao 2003).

During the UMDC Movement, "Zhiqing" was the collective identity allocated to the group of over 16 million[2] people. In 1979 when the central government called a halt to the UMDC Movement, most of the 16 million members returned to the city and the Zhiqing group was dissolved accordingly. In the city, these individuals found themselves in a marginalized situation as surplus labour, and struggled to re-establish a preferable position in urban society. Zhiqing's predicament in the post-movement era is vividly illustrated by the commonly acknowledged appellation, "the lost generation".

Over 30 years have passed since Zhiqing's critical life transition. We are in a more objective position to reflect on the genesis of this "lost generation" and its consequences. A primary task is to clarify specificities and implications of that identity loss by carefully reviewing the relevant socio-historical context.

2   *Finding the "lost generation"*

As a result of the UMDC Movement, Zhiqing's life trajectory formed a circuit between the city and the countryside. One of its significant implications is that Zhiqing were situated in a bidirectional exclusion from the countryside where they were sent to and into which they had never really integrated, and from the city which had changed dramatically while they were away and which treated them as aliens when they returned. In other words, Zhiqing had lost the sense of belongingness ever since the beginning of the UMDC Movement.

The allocated group identity was a manifestation of the particularly equalitarian ideology of the UMDC Movement. In fact, those 16 million group members were from various family backgrounds and hence were never a monolithic community. No wonder these individuals would have disparate life trajectories once the coercive power ceased to intervene. In fact, Zhiqing have lived dispersedly as unrelated individuals since the end of the UMDC Movement. Moreover, ingroup strata became explicit and intensified in the post-movement era due to the successive socio-cultural transformations triggered by the Reform and Open policy. To put it simply, the disintegration of the Zhiqing group and differentiation within it led to the problematization of the group identity.

Therefore, the topic of identity loss can be understood from the above two aspects: the confusion of belongingness, and the problematization of Zhiqing identity. The complexity lies in the dynamic nature of the Zhiqing identity. The group–individual tension is inherent in every collective identity. Zhiqing identity is special for the changing dynamics of this tension. The following quotations provide an example.

Interviewer: What is your perspective on the "Zhiqing" identity?
Interviewee 29:   It used to have a sort of particular meaning and significance. Now it is just like a drop of water that falls into the sea, disappearing without a trace and assimilating with the rest, thus it has lost its particularity.
Interviewer: Many interviewees while being asked about their perspectives on the "Zhiqing" identity or their personal identities declare that their identities are not special or that they have not seriously thought about their identities.
Interviewee 27:   Yes. The "Reform and Open" started from the negation of the Up to the Mountains and Down to the Countryside Movement . . . the entire 1980s and 1990s were about denouncing this movement. In this circumstance, most people were lost, feeling depressed and confused. Our ideals and enthusiasm turned out to be completely wrong!

The two interviewees perceive the Zhiqing identity from different perspectives. The first interviewee stresses Zhiqing's individualized way of life ("a drop of water in the sea") to justify why she thinks that Zhiqing identity "has lost its particularity". The second interviewee highlights socio-historical changes as the main reason for the widespread feeling of being "lost, depressed and confused" among Zhiqing. Interviewees' different perceptions indicate that the termination of the UMDC Movement marked two distinct stages of Zhiqing's identification process: the movement stage when the collective identity was assigned to group members, and the post-movement stage when the same collective identity was subject to individuals' interpretation and performance. Apparently, the group-identity tension has worked differently in the two periods.

In addition to the dynamic tension, the Zhiqing identity is also featured for its essential duality. As a social identity, its structural characteristics are dependent upon particular historical conditions and are subject to ever-changing social forces. At personal level, the Zhiqing identity has significant psychological implications and effects. A vivid example is the so-called "Zhiqing complex" which binds scattered and stratified individuals together as an "invisible" community that would become salient on occasions such as Zhiqing's get-togethers and thematic activities.

To summarize, it is necessary to investigate the above-illustrated two facets of the identity loss (belongingness confusion and problematized group identity) and the specificities of the Zhiqing identity (dynamic group–individual tension and structural-psychological duality). In doing so, this book hopes to retrieve the "lost generation" in history, society and individuals' minds. To achieve this, the writers combine diachronic and synchronic perspectives to form a two-pronged approach. The historical analysis in Chapter 2 will focus on diachronic changes to depict Zhiqing's life course and locate this particular generation in the social history. In Chapters 3 and 4, the social psychological analysis will analyse the structural and psychological features by comparing two distinct stages of Zhiqing's identification process. Three key questions are raised as follows: 1 what is Zhiqing's position in history, or who are Zhiqing historically?; 2 what did the Zhiqing identity mean to individuals during the UMDC Movement and how do they feel and think now?; 3 how have individuals been coping with changes in their identification processes?

1.2 Identity: group membership configured in time

In this book, identity is conceptualized within the domain of social psychology in accordance with the structural-psychological duality of the research object. Particularly, Henri Tajfel's social identity theory is chosen for its dynamic view of social groups and identities.

4 *Finding the "lost generation"*

At Bristol University, Henri Tajfel carried out his research on intergroup conflicts and social basis for prejudice and discrimination. From the beginning of his career, Tajfel had sought to establish an approach different from the personality expository model, with particular emphasis on group processes and intergroup relations. In fact, it is fair to say that the entire social identity theory is based on his conceptualization of social groups.

1.2.1 Social groups as processes

Taking a dynamic view, Tajfel (1982, 485) argued that "social groups are not 'things'; they are processes"; moreover, as processes, social groups only "come to life when their potential designations as such have acquired a psychological and behavioural reality". Tajfel's student John C. Turner (1982, 15) further interpreted the "psychological and behavioural reality" by arguing that:

> [A] social group can be defined as two or more individuals who share a common social identification of themselves or, which is nearly the same thing, perceive themselves to be members of the same social category. This definition stresses that members of a social group seem often to share no more than a collective perception of their own social unity and yet this seems to be sufficient for them to act as a group.

Instead of asking "what are social groups?", Tajfel and Turner sought to answer "how does a social group come into being?" and "what conditions make a group exist and maintain as the same group?" Compared with static and essentialist theories, Tajfel's and Turner's constructionist and dynamic perspective fits better with the study of the identity of Zhiqing for the following reasons:

1 the constructionist perspective emphasizes the group-forming process as well as the related conditions, hence it highlights the significance of historical, social and cultural contexts in which the Zhiqing group have been situated;
2 the dynamic view of group as processes enables the comprehension of diachronic changes of those conditions and contexts;
3 Turner's argument suggests an internal approach, through which implications and influences of the Zhiqing group and the Zhiqing identity could be explained from Zhiqing's own point of view.

1.2.2 Socially determined cognitive construction

In social identity theory, the identity of a specific social group is defined as the group membership that has normative efficacy on every member of that group. Another key concept identification is described as the process of group-identity configuration through which the group and the group membership are configured simultaneously in time and in situations. Based on these two concepts, Tajfel and his colleagues build the framework of social identity theory (see Figure 1.1). At the bottom of the framework are the three foundational presuppositions.

Presupposition 1: group-individual continuum

As a synthesis of its two parent disciplines, social psychology aims to discover underlying psychological mechanisms through which social influences are internalized by individuals and then work inwardly on their cognitions, attitudes and behaviours. One particular linkage that Tajfel found was self-concept, which he utilized to discuss the slippery object of identity. He carried out a series of minimal group experiments[3] to discover the critical mechanism that "switches on" the "group mode" self-concept which then leads to individuals' belongingness to the whole group as well as their compliance with group norms. This "group mode" self indicates Tajfel's belief in a fundamental discontinuity between an individual as a unique person and the same individual as a group member. Between the two extremes is the so-called "group-individual continuum", the implication of which is elaborated as follows:

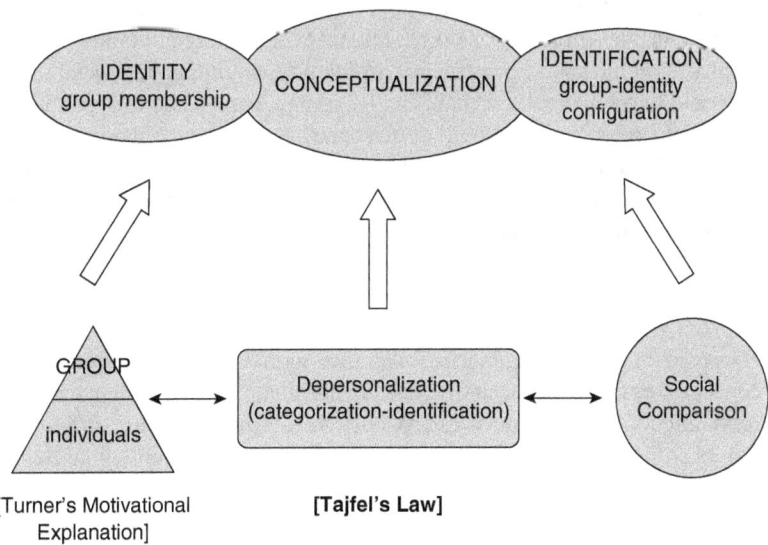

Figure 1.1 Structure of social identity theory

6 *Finding the "lost generation"*

The fundamental difference is that the individual's very conception of self changes to partake of the common attributes of an historically originated, socially determined and culturally and situationally constructed social group.

(Tajfel, 1982, 33)

On knowing the fundamental difference between the "group mode" self and the "individual mode" self, John Turner further argues that, "as category memberships become salient, there will be a tendency to exaggerate the differences on criteria dimensions between individuals falling into distinct categories, and to minimize these differences within each of these categories" (Turner 1982, 28). He named this tendency of ingroup-outgroup meta-contrast as "Tajfel's Law", which reveals its essentiality in the entire theoretical structure. Following Tajfel, Turner went a step farther by pointing out the evaluational implication of the meta-contrast:

[O]nce individuals define themselves or are defined by others as members of a category, there will be strong motivational pressure for them to assume that its characteristics are positive and even interpret as positive those designated as negative by outsiders.

Turner provided one explanation for the driving force of dynamism within the group-individual continuum as well as motivations for individuals' cognitive and behavioural compliance with the ingroup-outgroup meta-contrast. In this sense, Turner's motivational explanation equilibrates Tajfel's emphasis on the social construction of identity and integrates social influence and psychological mechanism. Tajfel and Turner laid the foundation of the integrated social-individual/structural-psychological theorization of identity. Their main arguments will be used in Chapters 3 and 4 of this book for interpreting the form and functioning of the Zhiqing identity and individuals' identification behaviours.

Presupposition 2: depersonalization

"Depersonalization" summarizes the transformation of a person's self-concept from the unique individual to the homogenized group member. As defined in social identity theory, once the ingroup-outgroup differentiation becomes salient, individuals undergo a process where they gradually think and behave consistently with others in the same group, turn into interchangeable representatives of the group's common attributes, and eventually become identical to each other. "Common attributes", as defined by Tajfel, derive from prototypes and norms of the certain group. Therefore,

Finding the "lost generation" 7

depersonalization is the process where individuals acquire and practise group norms and prototypes, which eventually result in the homogeneity of those individuals' ideas, attitudes and behaviours.

Social identity theorists also stated that prototypes and norms only come into force when categorical difference is perceived under social comparison circumstances such as group competition. This means that the depersonalized self is a latent state and that it is contextually salient just like group prototypes and norms. In other words, depersonalization does not mean permanent elimination of the unique individuality (personality, initiatives, etc.). It should be regarded as a threshold of the group mode of life.

The depersonalization presupposition has important implications for the study of Zhiqing's identity:

1   it is necessary to distinguish group norms and prototypes perceived and practised by Zhiqing themselves, and those understood by outgroup members and the whole society, especially socio-cultural connotations attached to the latter;
2   in historical, social and cultural senses, the Zhiqing identity is an imprint left on the entire group, while for individual group members, it is perceived and performed in particular ways;
3   the depersonalization process was activated twice at different historical times and in different ways. Thus it is vital to consider contextual shifts rendered by this circuit by comparing Zhiqing's rural lives during the UMDC Movement and their urban lives after the movement.

Presupposition 3: social comparison

If depersonalization is the underlying mechanism of the transition from the unique individual to the interchangeable representative of norms and prototypes, social comparison is an external force of the depersonalization process. In social identity theory, social comparison is the pervasive influence that gives rise to categorization and ingroup-outgroup meta-contrast. Consequently, already categorized individuals would enforce, protect and comply with the meta-contrast for the sake of their self-esteem because members' self-esteem is secured by the positive distinctiveness of the group in comparison with other groups.

The third presupposition is the prerequisite for the other two because social comparison provides the original impetus of group-individual differentiation and the depersonalization process. As Figure 1.1 shows, within this theory the psychological perspective is integral with the emphasis on social structural forces. The group-identity configuration as individuals' cognitive construction of their group and their group membership is by

8 Finding the "lost generation"

no means a self-contained process. It is activated by social forces (social comparison and social categorization) and realized through the socially determined mechanism of depersonalization.

1.2.3 The integrated group-identity configuration

As mentioned earlier, identification is the process in which the group and the identity (group membership) are simultaneously configured in time and in situations. This group-identity configuration process is composed of and realized by three consecutive procedures: social comparison, social categorization and social identification (see Figure 1.2).

Social comparison

Social comparison is the initial driving force. Its mechanism and consequences are illustrated by Tajfel's Law and Turner's motivational explanation. Under the effect of social comparison, scattered and unrelated individuals are divided into different categories and are given their respective categorical memberships. However, categorical memberships are still a formal differentiation and hence have no normative efficacy to individuals.

Social categorization

Social categorization is the key stage where group norms and prototypes emerge and solidify. As a result, the formal differentiation becomes concrete

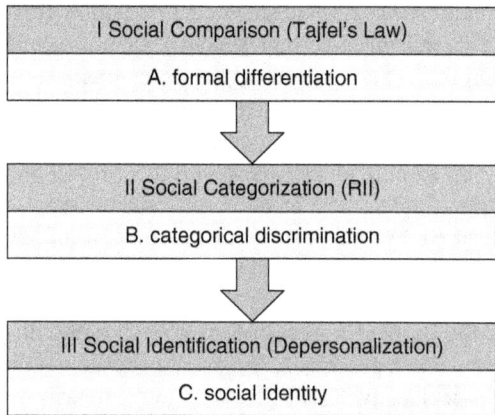

Figure 1.2 Consecutive procedures of identity formation

and intensified, and results in group-oriented judgements – namely, ingroup favouritism and intergroup discrimination. For social identity theorists, the critical questions are what gives rise to the emergence of norms and prototypes, and how do they come into force?

In accordance with Tajfel's and Turner's principles, attributes that qualify as norms and prototypes of a certain group should be those that serve the purpose of maximizing the group's distinctiveness in social comparisons. The practical criterion is how accessible and fit an attribute is in terms of realizing this ultimate purpose. As is defined by Rupert Brown (2000, 268–277), the accessibility and fitness are contingent upon the nature of the immediately preceding events, the personal disposition of the perceiver, and the current task or goal of the person (accessibility), as well as physical proximity, similarity, interdependence of fate and perceptual distinctiveness of certain people (fitness).

The actual functioning of norms and prototypes is in fact the issue of the mechanism of social categorization. With regard to this question, Tajfel put forward the Referent Information Influence (RII),[4] which he used to expound the inductive and deductive side of social categorization. As was described by John Turner (Tajfel 1982, 31–32), RII was essentially a running cycle formed by three consecutive stages:

1   Individuals define themselves as members of a distinct social category.
2   Individuals form or learn the stereotypic norms of that category. They ascertain that certain ways of behaving are criteria attributes of category membership. Certain appropriate, expected or desirable behaviours are used to define the category as different from other categories.
3   Individuals assign these norms to themselves in the same way that they assign other stereotypic characteristics of the category to themselves when their category membership becomes psychologically salient. Thus their behaviour becomes more normative (conformist) as their category membership becomes salient.

The above shown RII cycle starts from the inductive side, where certain attributes from individuals are inferred and stereotyped and highlighted as group norms and prototypes, and then leads to the deductive side, the assignment of these norms and prototypes to current and potential members.

By the stage of social categorization, categorical membership has had the potential to influence individual members' cognition and behaviour because of the effectiveness of group norms and prototypes formed and consolidated at this stage. However, this categorical membership is not an identity in its real sense until the potential is fully achieved in the next procedure.

10 *Finding the "lost generation"*

Social identification

According to social identity theory, the potential normative efficacy of categorical membership only comes into force when norms and prototypes are internalized by individual members. This critical internalization procedure is in fact the depersonalization process. As stated earlier, depersonalization is contextually salient and is rooted in the group-individual continuum. The actual process of depersonalization is achieved through three successive steps: homogenization, stereotyping and prototyping.

Although depersonalization is a psychological process, it is constantly and fundamentally influenced by social structural forces. Stereotypes and prototypes of a certain group are not simply value-free common attributes. According to Brown (2000, 290–306), due to the influence of social forces, stereotypes are then widely accepted as legitimate beliefs, expectancies and self-fulfilling prophecies. Hence researchers must be aware of their social constructive functions of legitimizing the status quo, especially group-based prejudices and social inequality. Besides, prototypes are also embedded in the context of social comparison and social categorization. To be more specific: in-group prototypes are usually positively evaluated while out-group prototypes are normally regarded as negative.

Therefore, the three steps of depersonalization have two implications to the discussion of the identity of Zhiqing:

1 acknowledged perceptions of Zhiqing, including associated evaluative connotations, are essentially stereotypes and prototypes;
2 it is crucial to pay attention to the implicit discourses and power relations by analysing how socially imposed stereotypes and prototypes influenced Zhiqing's lives as well as their attitudes towards and practice of the Zhiqing identity.

With regard to identification, two other issues that are relevant to this study are individuals' degree of identification and the reverse side of identification. According to social identity theory, members' identification with their group is manifested by their commitment, group solidarity and group conformity. Using the example of the reunion of East and West Germany, Brown (2000, 331) summarized three critical influences: legitimacy of the status difference, permeability of group boundaries, and stability of the macro-environment. He also argued that people who are in illegitimate, impermeable and unstable conditions have the highest degree of identification, and vice versa. Brown's argument reflects that members' degree of identification depends fundamentally on the status of their group in social comparisons. For this study, it is vital to notice that Zhiqing's degree of identification cannot be generalized but must be examined in specific circumstances. The discussion has to be in the context of Zhiqing's relationship with other social groups (urban citizens and farmers) at particular times.

Members with a very low degree of identification may distance themselves from other members and any symbolic and behavioural representative of the group, or simply leave the group if it is possible. This reverse side of identification is pertinent to those whose group memberships have incurred inferior positions or negative consequences. In reality, however, individuals' choices are often restricted by resources and adjusted by their risk assessments. Thus they would normally apply coping strategies to alleviate negative effects or feelings rather than challenging the established hierarchical system. A common strategy is relative deprivation. By switching the object or adjusting the scope of social comparison, members of an inferior group could achieve preferable outcomes of comparison and thereby manipulate the feeling of deprivation. Zhiqing is a disadvantaged group in Chinese society for historical reasons. The use of coping strategies would constitute an important aspect of an individual Zhiqing's identification behaviours.

1.2.4 Understanding Zhiqing in time and in context

To summarize: social identity theory defines both social group and identification as processes which would come into existence only when the potential normative efficacy of group membership is internalized by individual members. This dynamic and configuring nature means that social identities can never be "assigned to" individuals, but are always acquired by them in time and in context.

Within the framework of social identity theory, the Zhiqing group, the Zhiqing identity and individual members' identification are analysed in the context of social comparison and social categorization, guided by two rationales, Tajfel's Law and Turner's motivational explanation, and the conceptualization of group-identity configuration as well as the above-illustrated theoretical principles. Special attention will be given to several issues highlighted in this chapter, including the difference between social evaluation and Zhiqing's own perceptions, the temporal and contextual salience of the Zhiqing identity, socially constructed stereotypes and prototypes, and influences from social discourses and powers.

It is also necessary to clarify the limit of the chosen theoretical framework. Social identity theory would be inadequate when social comparison is not the dominant factor. This indicates that once the research emphasis shifts, to interpersonal relations for instance, Zhiqing's identity issues could be interpreted from other theoretical perspectives.

12 *Finding the "lost generation"*

Notes

1 Some historians like Ding Yizhuang (1998b) traced the UMDC Movement back to the mid-1950s. In this way, they included rural youth who returned to their home villages to undertake agricultural labour much earlier than urban youth. The latter were known as Zhiqing, whereas the rural youth were called Returning-home Zhiqing (Huixiang Zhiqing 回乡知青). The historical review in Chapter 2 of this book explains differences between Zhiqing and Huixiang Zhiqing. A major aim of this research is to review the adaptations Zhiqing experienced during and after the UMDC Movement in rural and urban societies, and discuss effects of these adaptations on Zhiqing's identification processes and behaviours. Different from ordinary Zhiqing, Huixiang Zhiqing were originally from the countryside, hence they are not included in this research.
2 Historians disagree as to the exact number of Zhiqing. This research adopts the number of 16 million based on Liu Xiaomeng's (1998b) calculation of urban youth who went to the countryside from 1962 to 1979.
3 See the rationale and design of minimal group experiments in Tajfel 1970.
4 In his article, Turner also compares major differences between RII, Normative Influence (NI) and Informational Influence (II). See more details in Tajfel 1982, 31–32.

2 Linking Zhiqing's life trajectories to social history

This chapter[1] reviews the life trajectory of the Zhiqing generation in the historical context. Based on Glen H. Elder's (1999, 2003; Giele and Elder 1998) life course approach, the Zhiqing generation is divided into three cohorts according to socio-historical factors and their respective demographic characteristics. The chapter thus addresses the question "who are the Zhiqing historically?" by illustrating the embeddedness of Zhiqing's life trajectories in the related history.

2.1 A brief history of the UMDC Movement

2.1.1 Pre-movement phase: 1953–65

The problems of an overheated economy became acute from 1953. One of the major issues was a low employment rate among the youth. To alleviate the pressure, the state encouraged rural youths who had just graduated from urban schools and universities to go home and join agricultural production.[2] Besides the unemployment issue, developing agricultural cooperatives was another important economic factor. In *The Climax of Socialism in Rural China* (《中国农村的社会主义高潮》) (General Office of the CCP Central Committee, 1956), Mao Zedong kept calling upon young people to resettle in the countryside and contribute to rural development, which he described as a way of serving the nation and self-achievement.[3]

Under these circumstances, youth reclamation teams emerged first as a voluntary and personal act. Then as a model, it spread quickly around the country, driven and guided by the Central Committee of the Communist Youth League. Two often-cited examples were the Beijing Youth Voluntary Reclamation Team (北京市青年志愿垦荒队) and the Shanghai Youth Voluntary Reclamation Team (上海市青年志愿垦荒队).[4] Nevertheless, the trend soon ended in 1956 because of economic difficulty and, more importantly, due to the failure of urban youth to adapt to intensive farm work and harsh conditions (Ding 1998b, 60–68).

Huixiang Zhiqing and members of youth reclamation teams could be seen as Zhiqing's predecessors. When Zhiqing went to the countryside later on, they faced the same urban–rural gap and similar practical problems. However, the history of the UMDC Movement shows that many of the policies and administrative arrangements of this early phase were still in use during the movement. This indicates that the dilemmas of those predecessors continued to be unresolved structural issues that had determined the direction and final results of the UMDC Movement long before its actual termination.

The unemployment issue, for example, followed a cycle that largely echoed fluctuations in the national economy. Yet it was complicated because it was not a purely economic problem, but was profoundly affected by social, political and particularly ideological influences. According to dominant ideologies then, young people, Huixiang Zhiqing and Zhiqing, were to devote themselves to rural development using their knowledge and skills. In reality, this normalized urban-to-rural migration had in fact become a measure of shifting socio-economic pressures to the vast and underdeveloped countryside. Consequently, a whole generation of educated young people was turned into simple labourers, which was simply a huge waste of human and educational resources. Again, for ideological reasons, this was an unspoken truth which was often shown in an ironic way, that is, "educated youths were less capable than illiterate peasants" (Ding 1998b, 63). Fundamentally, this was the result of the low productivity but at that particular time, young people's incapability and reluctance were simply regarded as the weakness and individualism of the bourgeoisie.[5]

1956 arrived, a key year when mobilizing youth to the countryside was adopted as a conventional method to ease urban unemployment after a few years of trial. The Political Bureau of the Chinese Communist Party (CCP) Central Committee (中共中央政治局) issued an "Outline of National Agricultural Development from 1956 to 1967 (draft)" (1956年到1967年全国农业发展纲要[草案]) on 23 January 1956. In Article 30, it says that graduates of urban secondary and primary schools, except for those who had managed to enter into further studies and those who had found jobs in the cities, should respond to the call and go into the countryside and up the mountains to join agricultural production and participate in the great cause of socialist agricultural construction. For the first time, "down to the countryside and up to the mountains" (下乡上山) appeared in an official document as a set term, just a different word order from the later well-known expression, "up to the mountains and down to the countryside" (上山下乡).

Implementation of the UMDC was halted in 1958 because of the Great Leap Forward. Then the number of unemployed urban youths reached 2 million in 1962[6] and the UMDC work was put onto the agenda again. In

October of the same year, the Agriculture and Forestry Office of the State Council (国务院农林办) held the Reporting Conference of Resettling Urban Redundant Staff and Young Students in State Farms, Forest Farms, Pastures and Fisheries (关于国营农林牧渔场安置家居大中城市精简职工和青年学生的汇报会议). Zhou Enlai delivered a speech in which he emphasized the effectiveness of mobilizing the urban population in the countryside to solve the problem of surplus labour in the city. At this meeting, the Leading Group of Resettlement Work of Agriculture and Forestry Office (农林办安置领导小组) was founded, which was the predecessor to the Leading Group Office of Zhiqing UMDC (知识青年上山下乡领导小组办公室).

The Leading Group Leaders Meeting of Resettlement Work for Urban Redundant Staff and Young Students (城市精简职工和青年学生安置工作领导小组长会议) was held in Beijing from June to July 1963. The report of this meeting was officially issued by the Central Committee of the CCP and the state in August 1963. Through key statements of the report it could be seen that relevant policies were changing due to different circumstances. For example, the eligible age went down from 18 to 16; the main resettlement destinations shifted from state farms to production teams; urban redundant workers were replaced by secondary school graduates (those who had failed to enter into higher education or those who could not find jobs) as the object of mobilization; these young students were supposed to develop into new peasants equipped by both knowledge and socialist ideals, with the education and influences they received from the poor and lower middle-class peasants (贫下中农) and collective farm workers (Gu 1997a, 38–40).

The state issued the "Decision on mobilizing and organizing urban Zhiqing to participate in socialist construction in the countryside (draft)" (关于动员和组织城市知识青年参加农村社会主义建设的决定[草案]) on 16 January 1964. The Leading Group of Zhiqing UMDC (知识青年上山下乡领导小组) and the Resettlement Office (安置办) were set up, followed by the establishment of corresponding organizations at each administrative level.

The Leading Group held a work meeting in February 1965. In the report of this meeting, Zhou Enlai made several important statements: the UMDC work was significant in terms of cultivating revolutionary successors, eliminating the "three main differences" (worker–peasant, city–countryside, and brain work–manual work) and constructing the new socialist countryside; the state was responsible for young people's resettlement and livelihood in the countryside; mobilization and resettlement work should be brought into the integrated planning of the urban workforce; a 15-year plan should be drawn up carefully (Gu 1997a, 60–64). This meeting marked the end of the pre-movement phase which, according to the above historical resources, had gone through the following stages:

16　*Linking Zhiqing's life trajectories to social history*

1　1953–57: secondary and primary school graduates were encouraged to go back to their home villages or to form youth reclamation teams;
2　1958–59: mobilization and resettlement work was suspended during the Great Leap Forward;
3　1960–62: mobilization and resettlement work was reactivated; the main resettlement destination was state farms;
4　1963–65: production teams became the main destination, and mobilization and resettlement work was institutionalized and implemented as a long-term routine project by the CCP and the state.

The pre-movement phase proved a significant time of exploration. In those 12 years, sending educated young people to the countryside was adopted initially as a temporal measure for the unemployment issue but was later gradually normalized and institutionalized as routine work of the CCP and the state. More specifically, a set of mobilization and resettlement measures was established, which, as summarized by Ding (1998b), consisted of unified organization, rigorous planning and provision of material needs by the state. – for example, the resettlement plan was incorporated as part of the annual national economic plan, special organizations were established at different administrative levels, and a special fund was provided and planned by the state to provide resettlement fees (Ding 1998b, 236–241).

Guiding ideologies also emerged during this phase under the influence of competing socio-political powers. From the early 1960s, ultra-left ideologies started to take control over the UMDC work and turned it into a political movement. The Communist Youth League submitted the "Report on Organizing Urban Zhiqing to Engage in Socialist Construction in the Countryside" (关于组织城市知识青年参加农业社会主义建设的报告) to the Central Committee of the CCP in April 1964. This report stated clearly that mobilizing urban youths to go to the countryside was of great importance to the revolutionization of educated young people, and hence it ought to be carried out as an important political task. The implied ideology was: "Educated young people, as part of the petty bourgeoisie category, needed to reinvent themselves. The only way was to integrate with workers and peasants by engaging in manual labour . . . It was the first step in the revolutionization of these youth" (Ding 1998b, 241).

Finally, the Zhiqing group took shape during the pre-movement phase. It was differentiated from other social groups in terms of its exclusive rights and obligations. On the one hand, Zhiqing were entitled to a certain resettlement fee, which guaranteed their basic needs were met at the initial stage of resettlement, including grain for the first year, expenses related to new houses and farm tools.[7] On the other hand, when Zhiqing left their home cities for the countryside, their registered permanent residences were transferred

Linking Zhiqing's life trajectories to social history 17

simultaneously to the relevant production teams or farms. According to the Household Registration System and strict domicile control at that time,[8] they were literally forced to take root in the countryside and become real peasants.[9] Moreover, because of the economic and hierarchical significance of the household registration system, the identity change from urban youth to Zhiqing had fundamental significance for these young people's livelihoods and self-development.[10] A whole generation's destiny was changed completely. Therefore, in ideological, political and social senses, the term "Zhiqing" had acquired its special meaning by the end of this pre-movement phase. It was no longer associated with the original but general meaning of "youths who have had a certain amount of knowledge" (Zhishi qingnian 知识青年), but was consolidated as a proper noun that referred specifically to young urban students who were sent to the countryside and were supposed to take root there and become agricultural labourers thereafter.

2.1.2 The UMDC Movement: 1967–81

Universities and secondary schools were all shut down after the commencement of the Cultural Revolution in May 1966. Later, the Central Committee of the CCP and the State Council issued the "Notification of University Entrance Examination Reform" (关于改革高等学校招生考试办法的通知) on 13 June 1966 and "Notification of University Enrolment Reform" (关于改革高等学校招生工作的通知) on 24 July 1966. According to the two documents, university and college enrolment was suspended until 1970.[11] Most secondary school students went back to their classes, but universities and colleges were still closed in November 1967. At the same time, the economy had experienced a 9.6 per cent decrease in the gross output value of industry and agriculture, while job recruitment had been suspended in most factories because of the social and political unrest. As a result, millions of secondary school graduates became surplus urban labour, causing enormous pressure in terms of employment and social stability.

To contain restless red guards and to solve socio-economic pressure in the city, the UMDC work was put back on the agenda. On 4 May 1967, *The People's Daily* published an editorial: "Zhishi Qingnian Must Integrate with Workers and Peasants" (知识青年必须同工农相结合). Later, on 9 July, it published another editorial, "Asserting the Right Direction of Zhiqing UMDC" (坚持知识青年上山下乡的正确方向). Some red guards like Cai Lijian (蔡立坚) and Qu Zhe (曲折) responded to the call and settled down in the countryside.[12] At that time, these volunteers did not realize that they had actually ushered in a nationwide movement. The entire process of the UMDC Movement can be divided into three main stages according to key years of policy changes: stage one (1967–69), stage two (1969–73) and

18 *Linking Zhiqing's life trajectories to social history*

stage three (1974–78), as well as a three-year epilogue (1978–81). Table 2.1 illustrates this development process.

Stage one: 1967–69

At this stage, the policy of "sending young people to the countryside" which during the former years was implemented as routine work, eventually turned into a movement. Under the pervasive influence of leftist ideologies, many activist students joined the movement out of genuine revolutionary aspirations. For others, going to the countryside was a testimony of their trustworthy political stance and loyalty to the Party and Chairman Mao.

New guiding ideology of the movement known as the "Re-education Theory" (再教育理论) also took shape and replaced slogans like "Revolutionization of the Youth" and "Revolutionary Successors". Before 1966, "revolutionization" was the ultimate motivation that encouraged Zhiqing to undertake the transition from educated urban citizens to simple labourers in the countryside. Compared with that, "Re-education" had a much stronger mandatory effect.

On 22 December 1968, *The People's Daily* published a report on the story of some students in Huining County (甘肃省会宁县) who volunteered to move to the countryside and participate in agricultural production. The reporter quoted Mao Zedong's special instruction:

Table 2.1 Numbers of Zhiqing (1962–79)

Year	Total	Production teams	Collective farms and production teams	State farms
Total	17,764,800	12,822,100	2,030,800	2,911,900
1962–66	1,292,800	870,600		422,200
1967–68	1,996,800	1,659,600		337,200
1969	2,673,800	2,204,400		469,400
1970	1,064,000	749,900		314,100
1971	748,300	502,100		246,200
1972	673,900	502,600		171,300
1973	896,100	806,400		89,700
1974	1,724,800	1,191,900	346,300	186,600
1975	2,368,600	1,634,500	496,800	237,300
1976	1,880,300	1,228,600	415,100	236,600
1977	1,716,800	1,137,900	419,000	159,900
1978	480,900	260,400	189,200	31,300
1979	247,700	73,200	164,400	10,100

Source: Table 3B from Liu 1998b, 863

It is necessary that Zhiqing go to the countryside and get re-educated by poor and lower-middle peasants (贫下中农). We should persuade urban cadres and other people to send their children who are secondary school and college graduates to the countryside to carry out the mobilization. Comrades in various rural areas should welcome them.

This "12/22 Instruction" soon spread across the country as the new slogan of the UMDC Movement. Under the effect of Mao's powerful command, the movement soon extended from big cities to smaller ones and towns. From 1967 to 1969, over 4.6 million urban youths joined the UMDC Movement (2.6 million in 1969), making the first climax stage of the movement (see Table 2.1). More importantly, the first few years of the UMDC Movement was a significant stage also for other reasons. It created the "Laosanjie" (Old Three Grades 老三届) subgroup whose members saw themselves as distinct from subsequent Zhiqing because of their active political stance and the exemplary role played by some model volunteers in the group. Besides, "Re-education theory" started to dominate the discourse field with the effect of leftist forces. Before that, confusing ideologies had resulted in different interpretations of the Zhiqing identity – for instance, "a new generation of educated peasants as contributors to socialist rural construction", "revolutionary youth as successors of the socialist course" and "petty bourgeoisie who ought to be re-educated in the countryside". Throughout the whole history of the movement, these three main connotations often fused together and manifested as one single Zhiqing identity, the ambiguity of which has been a main reason for individual Zhiqing's identity problems.

Stage two: 1969–73

In the second stage, inherent problems and practical difficulties in the UMDC Movement gradually emerged and intensified. Examples were issues like poor management of the resettlement fee and low participation of urban youth.

As is shown in Table 2.1, the number of Zhiqing started to fall in 1970, followed by a sharp three-year slump. Generally, Zhiqing lived in extreme poverty due to their incapability for adaptation and agricultural work. Their dependence aggravated the financial difficulties of the rural economy and intensified the rural–urban conflict. On the other hand, Zhiqing suffered from physical and psychological maladjustment. A few individuals were discriminated and even persecuted. According to Liu Xiaomeng's research, administrators at different levels emphasized mobilization and neglected planning and preparation; "re-education theory" was also accountable for Zhiqing's inferior social status (Liu 1998b, 275). In this sense, this low tide was a natural consequence of rapid expansion in the earlier stage.

Having noticed those problems, the central authorities sought to find solutions and motivate young people. While adjusting certain guidelines and methods, the state also issued new policies to provide educational and career opportunities for Zhiqing so as to improve their morale. In June 1970, the "Report on Recruitment (pilot) of Beijing University and Qinghua University" (北京大学、清华大学关于招生[试点]的请示报告) was approved. As a result, student recruitment at third-level education institutes was resumed based on a new principle of "integrated recommendation, approval and recheck" (群众推荐、领导批准、学校复审相结合). Every year from 1970, a few Zhiqing entered universities and colleges through this programme.[13] Then at the "National Planning Conference" (全国计划会议) in 1971, Zhiqing was included in the plan for job recruitment. Job quotas were assigned to individuals selected from candidates who were supposed to have recommendations from poor peasants and at least two years' work experience in the countryside.

In the short term, these new methods proved effectively comforting for the hope they indicated, yet they also left incentive for instability and uncertainty in the movement and the Zhiqing group. First, individuals tried every way to compete for the small quota, which caused disputes and chaos in the Zhiqing group. Second, individual cases of fraud and rent seeking had a destructive influence on the administration and reputation of the movement. Lastly and fundamentally, the adjustment of certain policies could not address the structural problems of the UMDC Movement. Even these useful methods were interrupted and abandoned later because of a series of political incidents. Consequently, the first crisis hit the UMDC Movement just after the low tide.

In December 1972 Li Qinglin, a school teacher from a small town in Fujian, wrote a letter to Mao Zedong in which he expressed his concerns for the future of his two sons in the countryside.[14] Surprisingly, he received a reply from Mao Zedong as well as 300 yuan RMB in April 1973. In his letter, Mao wrote: "There are many similar issues in the country. Please allow us to address them through overall planning" (全国此类事甚多:容当统筹解决。). Because of this comment, the event became a transition of the UMDC Movement as it triggered a critical conference, the National Conference on the UMDC Work, which was held as a response to Mao's instruction for "overall planning".

The State Council held the National Conference on the UMDC Work (全国知识青年上山下乡工作会议) from 22 June to 7 August 1973. After this conference, important policy changes and concrete measures were implemented. Some of the significant adjustments included: favourable policies issued for those who were disabled, an only child or with particular circumstances to return home; the establishment of collectively owned farms and production

Linking Zhiqing's life trajectories to social history 21

teams for relocating Zhiqing; the release of a six-year plan to be implemented after the conference for overall organization of the UMDC Movement, which clarified four main forms of access to the city: job recruitment, university enrolment, conscription and promotion (Gu 1997a, 141–142).

The conference marked the end of the second stage of the UMDC Movement (1969–73). Zhiqing who went to the countryside during those five years were categorized as a specific subgroup: "Xinwujie" (The New Five Grades 新五届). In contrast to the former stage, stage two was a period of low uptake and adjustments. The low tide could be seen as a direct result of overheated mobilization and ill management of the first stage. Through the entire process of the UMDC Movement, it was obvious that fluctuations were in fact intensifications of inherent contradictions in the UMDC Movement, which were often manifested as unbalanced relations between population growth and economic development, the urban–rural gap, and rural construction, overall planning and policy adjustments. At a relatively earlier stage, the conference and subsequent adjustments still had certain effects in suspending the crisis. Because of this temporal effect, the UMDC Movement had a second climax at the beginning of its third stage.

Stage three: 1974–78

Over 7.6 million Zhiqing went to the countryside (over 1.7 million per year) during this phase. It demonstrated the effectiveness of adjustments after the National Conference on the UMDC Work.[15] However, some of the structural changes also indicated that from the beginning of its third stage, the UMDC Movement gradually deviated from its original purpose and moved towards its end.

This double effect was best illustrated by resettlement changes. During this third stage, resettlement destinations moved closer to the Zhiqing's home cities or even to suburban areas; relocation sites moved from production teams to production brigades and communes; new farms and brigades were established for Zhiqing (Liu 1998b, 439). Two new policies – the Zhuzhou Model (株洲模式) and the Leading Cadre System (干部带队制) – were implemented nationwide during this stage and fundamentally changed the trajectory of the UMDC Movement.[16]

The Zhuzhou Model was an innovation in the sense that mobilization and resettlement work was no longer the government's sole responsibility but was mainly organized by urban factories and mines of the Zhuzhou city where Zhiqing's parents worked, based on close cooperation between these workplaces and the villages. It showed clearly that to continue the UMDC Movement, the city had to play a more significant role and share the responsibility with the countryside. This indicates that the UMDC Movement had deviated from its origins, because initially a main objective was to transfer unemployed urban youth and alleviate related social conflicts in the city. On the other hand, the Leading Cadre System aimed at safeguarding Zhiqing's living standards and rights by sending "guardians" to stay with them in the countryside for a year. This new method was a direct response to Zhiqing and their parents' complaints. It showed that at this stage, the government became directly involved in reconciling the conflict between the Zhiqing group and rural society, which indicated the difficulty of Zhiqing's integration and the failure of the re-education theory.

In the meantime, more and more Zhiqing went back to the city through different channels, including favourable policies for disabled people and single children, as well as job, education and conscription opportunities. By 1976, over 7.3 million Zhiqing had left the countryside. As a result, the cohesiveness and morale of the Zhiqing group were seriously disrupted. For individuals, their revolutionary enthusiasm cooled as they stayed longer in the countryside. The authorities also found themselves in an awkward situation: they had to emphasize the availability of various returning channels while mobilizing urban youth to go to the countryside. To be more precise, the sent-down experience had turned into a compulsory yet temporal phase before job allocation and further education.

Different phenomena pointed to one simple truth: the UMDC Movement had gone off its designed track since the announcement of the iconic "12/22 Instruction". The UMDC Movement turned out to be a heavy financial burden on the state. Millions of young people became simple labourers who hardly used their knowledge or skills in the countryside. Most of the doctrinal slogans, such as "taking root" and "re-education" turned out to be empty talk, with Zhiqing's actual dependency upon the state, disillusion about political ideals and eagerness to come home. Just as pointed out by Liu (1998b, 461), "the UMDC Movement deviated from its original purposes. Leaders were stuck in a vicious circle". The situation worsened after the ultra-left "Gang of Four" took over in 1974.[17] In allusion to acute problems and crisis, Mao Zedong issued an instruction on 12 February 1967: "It might be better to carry out special research on the Zhiqing issue. [We] should first make preparations and then hold a conference to solve this issue."[18] This was known as the "2/12 Instruction", which initiated preparation for the Second National Conference on the UMDC Work.

The second conference took place in Beijing from 31 October to 10 December 1978. The Central Committee of the CCP released two documents: the "Minutes of the National Conference on the UMDC Work" (全国知识青年上山下乡工作会议纪要) and the "Trial Provisions about Several Issues of 'UMDC' by the State Council" (国务院关于知识青年上山下乡若干问题的试行规定) on 12 December. Some of the main resolutions included: 1 the UMDC Movement would be continued for the purpose of terminating it under appropriate circumstances; 2 the movement would be downsized gradually, and some qualified cities were allowed to stop mobilizing their urban youth; 3 resettling Zhiqing in production teams would be replaced by establishing Zhiqing farms and production teams with preferential policies; 4 Zhiqing in production teams would be relocated; and 5 cities and towns would be required to expand employment (Gu 1997a, 178–185). As indicated by these key resolutions, this conference sent out, to the whole country, a signal that the termination of the UMDC Movement had been put on the agenda. In reality, large numbers of Zhiqing in production teams started flocking into cities through channels that had opened after this conference. Zhiqing who went to the countryside from 1974 to 1978 were called "Houwujie" (the Post-Five Grade 后五届), a specific subgroup who witnessed significant changes in policies and measures.

From the "risk–adjustment–another risk–readjustment" cycle, reviewers could get a general understanding of the entire process of the UMDC Movement. It is also vital to notice transformations that happened internally. Just as the movement had its high tides and low tides, the spirit of the Zhiqing group also had its ups and downs. These explicit and implicit aspects of the movement were interrelated and were both embedded in the wider social historical context. Hence today, when we look back, we see clearly how Zhiqing's life trajectory had been woven into the macro-history.

Termination: 1978–81

The University/College Entrance Examination was resumed in 1977.[19] This reactivated Zhiqing's aspiration for higher education but also accelerated the disintegration of the Zhiqing group. In the meantime, the state started to resolve the Zhiqing issue through an economic approach. Deng Xiaoping expressed his thought of incorporating the Zhiqing issue into the overall planning of urban employment in March 1978. While the central leadership was looking for a less dramatic resolution, Zhiqing chose strike and protest to stake out their position.

Zhiqing at Jinghong Farm in Yunnan Province (云南省景洪农场) sent two joint letters to the State Council in October 1978. Two months later, a petition group of these Zhiqing arrived in Beijing, where they were received by Vice-Premier Wang Zhen and Minister for Civil Affairs Cheng Zihua.[20] The Yunnan Zhiqing's protests ceased for a while, but soon started again in January 1979. The trend of protest swept across 21 provinces and areas in February 1979. The state had to take a series of emergency measures to control the situation.²¹ Regulations were further relaxed, which led to a flow of Zhiqing en masse to the city in a short period. Only 247,000 Zhiqing went to the countryside in 1979, whereas the number of returned Zhiqing was nearly 4 million in the same year.

The Central Committee of the CCP and the State Council convened the National Conference on Labour Employment Work (全国劳动就业工作会议) in August 1980. After the conference, comprehensive solutions were applied to ensuring employment for Zhiqing in the cities.²² In 1981, most of the unemployed Zhiqing found jobs. The unemployment rate decreased from 5.4 per cent in 1979 to 3.8 per cent in 1981. Governments of each administrative level also went to great efforts to resolve the remaining problems of the UMDC Movement, such as making arrangements for disabled Zhiqing and married Zhiqing and their children, as well as calculating Zhiqing's working years and auditing UMDC funds.²³ The Zhiqing Office drafted the "Review and Summary of Zhiqing Work over 25 Years" (二十五年来知青工作的回顾与总结) in October 1981. It summarized important aspects of the UMDC Movement, including its origins, processes, faults and experience. At the end of 1981, the Zhiqing Office was incorporated into the State Labour Bureau, followed by provincial and municipal governments. This marked the official termination of the UMDC Movement as well as the beginning of a post-movement era. The latter has been a difficult ongoing journey of recovery and adaptation for Zhiqing and the whole society in both material and spiritual senses.

2.1.3 Summary

The UMDC Movement was a unique event in human history. As was shown in the above historical review, it was characterized by its long timespan, wide scope, multiple changes, and complex background and factors, as well as its contradictory nature. Its origins, development and termination were all rooted in structural and fundamental contradictions of Chinese society as well as the evolution of these contradictions under different historical circumstances.

The above review reproduces the social-historical context in which Zhiqing's lives were embedded. Bernstein (1977), one of the earliest Western Zhiqing scholars,²⁴ observed the complexity and argued that while reviewing and evaluating the UMDC Movement, a researcher should consider alternative options and compare the cost-benefit ratios of these options.²⁵ As the first generation of the People's Republic of China (PRC), Zhiqing's life transitions echoed most of the turning points of the nation's history, which has made them a special generation in both a demographic and historical senses.

2.2 The making of the Zhiqing generation: a life course analysis

2.2.1 Glen H. Elder's life course approach

Glen H. Elder was known as a founder of the life course approach of human development research. After joining the University of North Carolina at Chapel Hill in the 1960s, he started to combine the traditional life span theory and life cycle theory with an historical dimension and put forwards the life course theory. This new theory enables researchers of human development to locate their research objects in their life trajectories and social history as well as in the synthesis of the two. In *Methods of Life Course Research*, Giele and Elder (1998, 22) gave their definition of life course: "Life course refers to a sequence of socially defined events and roles that the individual enacts over time." Angela O'Rand (1998, 72–73) further elaborated this broad definition by explicating:

> The life course studied in analytical time reveals transitions, trajectories, careers, cohorts, and generations. In perspective time, the life course is presented as identities, actions, and choices – as well as recollections and retrospections – constrained by the present. In perspective time, the future and the past are constrained by the immediate historical and structural circumstances of persons as actors. In the present, actors reflect on their past lives and consider the "present understood past" (Cohler, 1982). Life reviews and retrospectives repeatedly reveal how the developing individual reconsiders and reinterprets the past in light of the vantage point of the present.

As a time concept, life course is constituted by three aspects: developmental trajectory and transitions, individual life course, and social pathways. In specific research, life course is often measured by the following interrelated indicators: timing and sequence of life transitions and psychosocial stages, duration of a particular status, birth cohorts and age grades, and social changes. In this particular research, the life course approach is chosen for its fitness and efficacy in analysing the developmental process of the Zhiqing generation as well as its connectedness with UMDC Movement.

2.2.2 Three cohorts of the Zhiqing generation

As is shown in the above historical review, the UMDC Movement (1967–81) was composed of three stages. Hence the Zhiqing generation were divided into three subgroups: Laosanjie, Xinwujie and Houwujie. The following analysis treats these historically formed subgroups as cohorts because for the Zhiqing, historical influences were much more important than biological factors such as birth years. Table 2.2 illustrates key features of the three subgroups, including their birth years, positions in history, and timing of key role transitions.

The main research principles summarized by Elder (1999, 304–312) are applied to detailed analysis of the three cohorts.

1 The life course of individuals is embedded in and shaped by the historical times and events they experience over their lifetime;
2 The developmental impact of a succession of life transitions or events is contingent on when they occur in a person's life;
3 Social-historical influences are expressed through the network of shared relationships;
4 Individuals construct their own life course through the choices and actions they take within the opportunities and constraints of history and social circumstances.

Laosanjie

Laosanjie's birth years ranged from 1947 to 1952. They went to the countryside between late 1967 and early 1969. They were secondary school students from six grades: the old grade three of senior high school (Laogaosan 老高三), the old grade two of senior high school (Laogao'er 老高二), the old grade one of senior high school (Laogaoyi 老高一), the old grade three of junior high school (Laochusan 老初三), the old grade two of junior high school (Laochu'er 老初二), and the old grade one of junior high school (Laochuyi 老初一). After the explosion of the Cultural Revolution, these six grades of secondary school graduates were stuck at home. When the CCP and the state reactivated the UMDC, they went to the countryside as one batch over less than two years. This cohort is characterized for the following features:

Table 2.2 Cohort, year of birth and key years in the context of the UMDC Movement

Year cohort	1962	1966	1969	1973	1976	1978	1979	1981	1992	2012
Laosanjie (1947–52)	10–15	14–19	17–22	21–26	24–29	26–31	27–32	29–34	40–45	60–65
Xinwujie (1953–57)	5–9	9–13	12–16	16–20	19–23	21–25	22–26	24–28	35–39	55–59
Houwujie (1958–62)	0–4	4–8	7–11	11–15	14–18	16–20	17–21	19–23	30–34	50–54

Linking Zhiqing's life trajectories to social history 27

1   Birth years and current age grade: within this cohort, the age difference could be six years, which is not seen in the other two cohorts. In 2012 when fieldwork for this book was conducted, the majority of them have retired, with only a very few executives still remaining in their positions.[26]
2   Population size: the figure of Laosanjie is about 4 million (see Table 2.1).
3   Timing of the UMDC: when Laosanjie went to the countryside, their average age was around 16 (with a few aged 14 or 20). Due to the Cultural Revolution, most Laosanjie (except the eldest – Laogaosan) did not finish secondary education. The younger they were, the less schooling they had. Besides, many of them were red guards in the city before they went to the countryside. This means that they could have had an identity transition from red guards to Zhiqing, which Xinwujie and Houwujie did not experience.
4   Duration at the countryside: Laosanjie stayed in the countryside for more than five years.[27] A great number of Laosanjie even stayed for around ten years. This means Laosanjie spent their entire youth and the beginning of adulthood in the countryside, which caused a serious structural lag in career, marriage, childrearing and other life events.
5   Life transitions and social changes: as shown in Table 2.2, Laosanjie experienced the establishment of the PRC and the institutionalization of socialism and economic construction from their infancy (0–2 in 1949) to childhood/late juvenile (10–15 years old in 1962, the end of the Second Five-Year Plan), the Cultural Revolution and the UMDC Movement from their late juvenile/early youth (14–19 in 1966) to late youth (29–34 in 1981), the implementation of the Reform and Open policy from their late youth (27–32 in 1979) to early middle age (40–45 in 1992) and to old age (60–65 in 2012).

Xinwujie

Xinwujie went to the countryside from 1969 to 1973. They were secondary school graduates of these five years. During the low tide of the UMDC Movement, Xinwujie witnessed various difficulties, fundamental problems and the first significant adjustment of UMDC policies and measures, but also benefited instantly from the relaxation of the job recruitment policy in 1971. By then, the first batch of Xinwujie had worked in the countryside for two years, which just met the criterion.

1   Birth years and current age grade: Xinwujie were born from 1953 to 1957. In 2012, they were in the 55–59 age group; in the subsequent five years, they will all retire.
2   Population size: Xinwujie has a similar population of 4 million.

28 Linking Zhiqing's life trajectories to social history

3 Timing of the UMDC: as graduates of secondary school, Xinwujie joined the UMDC Movement at around 16 years old. Age difference was smaller in this cohort. Nine years' basic education was their average education level.[28]
4 Duration in the countryside: due to policy changes from the early 1970s, many Xinwujie stayed for around two years and then returned to the city through various channels. The structural lag also impacted Xinwujie's lives, but not as severely as Laosanjie.
5 Life transitions and social changes: Xinwujie experienced the institutionalization of socialism and economic construction from their pre-school to childhood (5–9 years old in 1962), the Cultural Revolution and the UMDC Movement from their childhood/early juvenile (9–13 in 1966) to early youth (24–28 in 1981), the Reform and Open era from their early youth (22–26 in 1979) to late youth (35–39 in 1992) and to late middle age (55–59 in 2012).

Houwujie

Houwujie went to the countryside from 1974 to 1978. During these five years, the UMDC Movement deviated from its original track and gradually moved towards its end.

1 Birth years and current age grade: Houwujie were born around 1958 to 1962. They were in the 50–54 age group in 2012. In the ten years after 2012, Houwujie will all retire.
2 Population size: Houwujie has the largest population size of about 8.05 million. They comprised the second peak of the UMDC Movement from 1974 to 1977.
3 Timing of the UMDC: like Xinwujie, Houwujie were also new graduates of secondary schools. Compared with the former cohorts, they stayed in the countryside for a relatively shorter time because policies were more relaxed. As the youngest cohort, they were more competitive in job recruitment.
4 Duration in the countryside: under the new historical circumstances, Houwujie generally did not have the problem of structural lag.
5 Life transitions and social change: Houwujie experienced socialist economic construction during their pre-school (0–4 in 1962), the Cultural Revolution and the UMDC Movement from their pre-school/childhood (4–8 in 1966) to early youth (19–23 in 1981), the Reform and Open era from their early youth (17–21 in 1979) to late youth (30–34 in 1992) and to late middle age (50–54 in 2012).

Based on the above profile of the three cohorts, a more thorough life course analysis could be made, focusing on the four elements in Elder's analytic framework: cohort members' exposure to historical and social change, life chances, changing social economic statuses during their development processes, as well as interrelated lives.[29]

2.2.3 Exposure to socio-historical changes

In life course theory, socio-historical changes refer to changes that happened on institutional and structural levels and key turning points in history. For the Zhiqing generation, the Cultural Revolution, UMDC Movement and implementation of the Reform and Open policy are the three most significant historical events. Besides, the degree and the result of Zhiqing's exposure to socio-historical changes also depend upon their particular positions in historical time as well as the specific developmental stage they are in when each significant event occurred.

Tables 2.3, 2.4 and 2.5 present an outline of the three cohorts' locations both in historical time and in their respective developmental processes. Their exposure to every socio-historical change can be analysed based on this general notion.

Table 2.3 Average age and age range of each cohort during the Cultural Revolution (1966–76)

Key years average age	1966	1974	1976	Age range
Laosanjie	16	25	26	14–24/19–29
Xinwujie	12	19	21	9–19/13–23
Houwujie	6	14	16	4–14/8–18

Table 2.4 Average age and age range of each cohort during the UMDC Movement (1968–79)

Key years average age	1968	1973	1978	Age range
Laosanjie	19	24	29	16–27/21–32
Xinwujie	14	19	24	12–23/15–26
Houwujie	9	13	18	6–17/10–21

30 Linking Zhiqing's life trajectories to social history

Table 2.5 Average age and age range of each cohort since the Reform and Open era (1979–2012)

Key years average age	1979	1992	2012	Age range
Laosanjie	30	43	63	27–60/32–65
Xinwujie	24	37	57	22–55/26–59
Houwujie	19	32	52	17–50/21–54

The UMDC Movement

In the early 1960s, going to the countryside was not yet compulsory for urban youth. As juveniles, most Laosanjie were in school, were taught by the related ideologies and were familiar with all those role models. When they eventually joined the UMDC Movement just before or after Mao Zedong's "12–22 Instruction" (around late 1967 to early 1969), previous slogans like "revolutionization of the youth" were still in use. Being influenced by this former set of ideologies, most Laosanjie went to the countryside with the aspiration and belief that they would develop into successors of the socialist course and contributors to socialist rural construction.

This idealist characteristic has made Laosanjie a distinct cohort in the Zhiqing generation. In the early 1970s when Xinwujie went to the countryside, the "re-education theory" had become the dominant ideology of the UMDC Movement. Xinwujie's politically inferior status as the object of education resulted in their relatively negative experience and self-perception. Houwujie went to the countryside after the National Conference on the UMDC Work. Zhiqing's livelihood in the countryside was improved while regulations were also much relaxed. Hence they were less anxious but more pragmatic mainly due to an unspoken consensus: before any substantial change could happen, the "two years' sent-down experience" would be a necessary but temporary phase.

The Cultural Revolution

When the Cultural Revolution started in 1966, Laosanjie were around 14–19 years old. Most of them were red guards who created the nationwide turmoil. During the three years' climax of the Cultural Revolution (1966, 1967, 1968) made by Laosanjie, most of the Xinwujie were only primary school students. After 1968, young students were no longer the main force of the Cultural Revolution. Hence, Xinwujie's role in the Cultural Revolution was never as active and aggressive as Laosanjie's. For Houwujie, the Cultural Revolution was more like a childhood memory.

Reform and Open policy

In 1979, the state approved the establishment of four special economic zones at Shenzhen, Zhuhai, Shantou and Xiamen, which marked the beginning of the reform and open era. By then, most of the 17 million Zhiqing had returned to the city. Houwujie was the most competitive and adaptable cohort because of their age advantage. A similar age-related situation happened again in the 1990s when tens of millions of workers in state-owned enterprises were laid off. At that time, Houwujie were in their thirties, while Laosanjie and Xinwujie were over 40. Apparently, what Houwujie had was only a relative advantage within the Zhiqing group. The entire group was in a disadvantaged position in the job market mainly because of their insufficient education and skills.

To summarize, Xinwujie share certain common features with Laosanjie in terms of their exposure to major historical events. Houwujie is more special because of their later involvement in the UMDC Movement. The three cohorts' differentiated exposure to social historical changes show that the Zhiqing group is not a monolithic whole. It underwent an evolution every time a new cohort joined, at different historical times under different structural and institutional circumstances.

2.2.4 Life chances

For the Zhiqing generation, there are three main factors of life chance: education, structural lag and human resources.

Education

The years from 1949 to 1966 were a special period named the "17-year education" in the history of education of the PRC.[30] After the Cultural Revolution, universities, colleges and schools were all closed. In October 1967, the "Notification of Resuming Revolution in Classes" was released. Then during the Cultural Revolution, elementary and secondary education were reduced to nine or ten years.[31] Higher education stopped from 1966 until 1972, when university and college enrolment started again with the new selection criterion – the recommendation method. Then from 1972 to 1977, only a few worker-peasant-soldier students were admitted to limited majors like science, engineering and agriculture; moreover, higher education was condensed to three years or even two years. Compared with high school graduates before 1966, worker-peasant-soldier students were generally weaker in academic performance. In 1977, the University/College Entrance Examination resumed. In that year, over 5.7 million people sat the examination, yet only 273,000 were admitted to colleges and universities. In 1978, over 6.1 million sat the examination, among which 402,000 were enrolled.[32] In these two years, examinees' ages varied from 16 to 40. In 1979, the state adopted the screening criterion of "unmarried and under 25 years old" for registration for the examination.

Laosanjie was the cohort brought up under the 17-year education. The eldest group, Laogaosan, in this cohort finished secondary education by 1966. They are the subgroup that benefited the most from the 17-year education. The youngest group, Laochuyi, graduated from primary school in 1966 when all schooling was halted. Apart from extreme cases, most Laosanjie were secondary school students with seven or 11 years of education before they went to the countryside. Even though their education was interrupted by the Cultural Revolution, they had a more solid education foundation than Xinwujie and Houwujie. This was an advantage for Laosanjie in the University/College Entrance Examination. Nevertheless, from 1979, Laosanjie were no longer eligible to sit the examination because they had passed the upper age limit.

In 1966, Xinwujie were in the 9–13 age group. Only those born in 1953 and 1954 finished elementary education. So Xinwujie received only part of the 17-year education, had their secondary education during the Cultural Revolution and then went to the countryside after graduating from secondary school. With this educational background, Xinwujie did not have much advantage in the entrance examination in 1977 and 1978. Besides this, they also had an age problem like Laosanjie. Houwujie received all their elementary and secondary education during the Cultural Revolution. In the entrance examination, they were less competitive than other examinees such as new graduates and Laosanjie. They were more competitive in the job market than Xinwujie and Laosanjie because of their age advantage.

In general, the majority of Zhiqing were junior high school graduates. The quality of this limited education is still questionable because of the shortened length of schooling and the destructive effects of the Cultural Revolution. This education deficiency of a whole generation resulted in a huge gap of capable talent at the beginning of the Reform and Open era in the early 1990s. On one hand, this gave rise to a prevailing emphasis on diplomas and certificates at that time. On the other hand, Zhiqing's career development was badly impacted.[33] Later when mass layoffs began in the 1990s and 2000s, Zhiqing were again seriously affected because of their educational background and age. Therefore, it is clear that limited education in Zhiqing's early lives has had continuous effects on their later lives in terms of their access to life opportunities.

Structural lag

A main purpose of the UMDC Movement was to ease the pressure of unemployment by delaying new graduates' entrance into the job market. In this sense, the structural lag was an inherent side effect of the Movement. During the UMDC Movement, urban youth at the age of 16 were sent to the countryside. Taking it as the standard working age, the exact length of delay could be calculated. According to the regulation issued in 1971, Zhiqing who had stayed in the countryside for two years were eligible for job recruitment. Hence for most Zhiqing, two years was the shortest delay for employment.[34] Laosanjie was a special case. The youngest Laosanjie were 19 in 1971, so the shortest delay for them was three years, not two years. After the massive retreat in the late 1970s, the majority of returned Zhiqing were employed in 1980. By then, the eldest Laosanjie were 33, so the longest delay for Laosanjie was 17 years. Similarly, the longest delay for Xinwujie and Houwujie were 11 years and six years, respectively. Obviously, Laosanjie suffered from the most serious structural lag among the three cohorts. The structural lag was also reflected in other life events such as marriage and child-bearing, and was closely associated with the delay of Zhiqing's career development.

Human resources

Human resources were largely determined by Zhiqing's family background. According to Ding's (1998b, 275–298) analysis, Zhiqing came from various kinds of families, including urban workers, common urban citizens, common cadres, senior cadres, intellectuals and noted public figures, and untrustworthy classes like capitalists and rightists.

From the early 1970s, some Zhiqing from families of common cadres and urban citizens returned to the city earlier than their peers either through family connections or financial means. Zhiqing from senior cadre families came back to the city usually in the late 1970s or even in the early 1980s when their parents were reinstated. The rest of the society often criticized the misuse of family connections as "getting in through the back door" (Zou houmen 走后门) because Zhiqing from other families were relatively deprived.[35] Children of intellectuals and noted public figures were regarded as untrustworthy classes during the Cultural Revolution. Therefore, they often suffered discrimination, not to mention a lack of fair access to employment, higher education and other life chances. By comparison, Zhiqing from workers' families would easily get recommendations for those opportunities because of their trustworthy family background.

Zhiqing with certain family backgrounds enjoyed better life chances in the short term. Whether or not this turned into an advantage in the long run depended upon their social mobility and accumulation. This relates to the next topic: changes of socio-economic status. To summarize the above discussion on life chances: Zhiqing is a relatively disadvantaged group and generation in terms of their restricted access to life chances. This was a result of the short-term effect of the UMDC Movement – the structural lag as well as its long-term effects on Zhiqing's later life stages.

2.2.5 Changes of socio-economic status

Socio-economic status accumulates over time but develops in a spiral rather than a linear way. Its upgrade is contingent upon life chances, human agency, as well as social structural and institutional constraints. In the case of Zhiqing, the main constraints are caused by the above-mentioned three major historical events. Influences of the Cultural Revolution and the UMDC Movement are analysed in former sections. For the Reform and Open era in particular, two events that are worth mentioning here are Deng Xiaoping's trip to the southern regions in 1992, and structural reform in state-owned enterprises in the late 1990s.

In the early 1990s, Zhiqing were around their early thirties to early forties, a key stage of career advancement and wealth accumulation. However, Zhiqing failed to enhance their social economic status because of their education and skills inadequacy which then worsened due to the elevated social standard. As key signals of deepening economic reform, the above two events led to mass layoffs in the late 1990s and 2000s. As a result, Zhiqing experienced a retrogression of social economic status in their late thirties and late forties. In general, Zhiqing is a particular generation that suffered from a delayed and low beginning of social accumulation as well as social historical obstacles to their self-enhancement.

2.2.6 Interrelated lives

In Elder's analytic framework, human beings are not treated as isolated individuals but as interconnected by interpersonal and wider social networks. From this point of view, it is clear that Zhiqing's interrelated lives were enriched because of their unique UMDC experience.

Before they went to the countryside, Zhiqing's social relations were restricted to their connections with their parents and relatives, siblings, teachers, classmates and neighbours. The geographic space of their everyday life was within their home cities. During the UMDC Movement, Zhiqing's social relations expanded significantly in the countryside, where they worked and lived with their peers from other cities (or provinces[36]) and with peasants (or farm workers or soldiers) on a daily basis. After they returned to the city,

Zhiqing experienced job transfers, unemployment and re-employment, all of which led to wider and more complex social relations and networks. As a result, Zhiqing's interrelated lives were more complex when compared with the rest of the urban population who stayed in cities during the UMDC Movement. Now in their old age, Zhiqing's social activities have reduced a lot and have switched from professional oriented to more family oriented. Nevertheless, they still have abundant resources to develop networks with each other and with rural society. In fact, Zhiqing's gatherings and associations are widely seen nowadays mainly for their nostalgia for their youth and more availability of time and money.

2.3 Summary

Based on the historical review and life course analysis, answers to "who are Zhiqing historically?" can be summarized. This is a group created by the UMDC Movement and a generation whose life course has been shaped by the movement and its lasting effects. More thorough understanding, then, ought to take into consideration the following details about Zhiqing's position in history and their life experiences.

First of all, the fundamental importance of the UMDC Movement should not be reduced to mechanical coerciveness from political and ideological forces. What was pertinent to individual Zhiqing were embodiments of institutional and ideological designs in everyday life and individuals' own internalization of them. In other words, the profound, pervasive and enduring influence of the UMDC Movement lies in these concrete and living details, not in abstract policies or slogans. Therefore, the next two chapters will move from the grand narrative to Zhiqing's personal narratives to gather and analyse details in their lives and minds.

Second, the history of the UMDC Movement and the constitution of the Zhiqing generation suggest that the Zhiqing identity is not a static entity. Its social-cultural connotations constantly changed along the process of the UMDC Movement. An example of this is the change to the guiding ideology from "revolutionization of the youth" to "re-education theory", which fundamentally altered Zhiqing's social position and their self-perception. Hence to understand the making of Zhiqing generation, it is necessary to view Zhiqing's life experiences in the related socio-historical context from a diachronic perspective. This is what this chapter seeks to achieve.

Chapter 2 discusses the identity of Zhiqing from a combined historical and human developmental perspectives. Issues discussed in historical context, namely their exposure to historical changes, life chances, human agency and constraints as well as interrelated lives, will be further elaborated in Chapter 3 and Chapter 4 in the context of Zhiqing's life stories.

Notes

1 An historical review of the UMDC Movement has been published as an individual book chapter under the title "The Rise and Fall of the 'Up to the Mountains and Down to the Countryside' Movement: A Historical Review", in *Constructing the "Other"*, edited by Fan Hong, Peter Hermann and Daniele Massaccesi. Bremen: Europaeischer Hochschulverlag GmbH & Co. KG, 2013. The content in this chapter is revised.
2 Those rural youths were called Huixiang Zhiqing, a term that differentiates them from Zhiqing who later were provided with a resettlement fee and other preferential treatment when they were sent from cities to the countryside. To the wider society, Huixiang Zhiqing's return was justifiable for they were originally from the countryside. For themselves, however, this critical policy change denied their endeavour of pursuing professional jobs and urban life or simply urban citizenship.
3 In 1956, *The Climax of Socialism in Rural China* (《中国农村的社会主义高潮》) (General Office of the CCP Central Committee, 1956) was published. It included 104 notes written by Mao Zedong.
4 The Beijing team went to Luobei in Heilongjiang and established the first communist youth farm, which they named Beijing Village (Beijing zhuang 北京庄), in August 1955. The Shanghai team set up a Communist Youth Commune in De'an in Jiangxi a month later.
5 Ding Yizhuang argues that this was in fact where the guiding ideology of the UMDC Movement – "Re-education Theory" (再教育理论) – was derived from (Ding 1998b, 63).
6 The majority were redundant workers, secondary school graduates who had failed to enter higher education, and those who had not found jobs in the cities. For more details, see Ding (1998b, 194).
7 Usually, the money was distributed to corresponding farms, production teams and other receiving units and was not given to individual Zhiqing directly.
8 The "Household Registration Regulation" (户口管理条例) was approved by the Standing Committee of the National People's Congress on 9 January 1958 and has been implemented by the Ministry of Public Security ever since. According to this document, spontaneous rural-to-urban population flow is strictly prohibited. Since the urban residence (城市户口) was combined with commodity grain provision, once a Zhiqing transferred to rural residence, backflow became virtually impossible.
9 It was only when the ultra-leftist faction took control of the UMDC work after the commencement of the Cultural Revolution that the state enforced mandatory household relocation. When the UMDC work was operated by the CCP and the state as long-term routine work (1962–65), in order to mobilize as many urban youth as possible, the authorities had not applied any explicit stipulation or coercive measures in terms of Zhiqing's registered permanent residences (Zhao 2009, 500–508).
10 Problems arising from the unequal household registration system started to impact on Zhiqing's lives in the latter stage of their stay in the countryside. Accordingly, regaining their permanent urban residence certificates became a common major request when Zhiqing sought to return to the cities in the late 1970s.
11 In 1970, university enrolment resumed through the new method of recommendation. Students who entered into higher education from 1970 to 1976 were called "worker-peasant-soldier students".

Linking Zhiqing's life trajectories to social history 37

12 For more details on these early volunteers, see Gu 1997a, 111–115; and Liu 1998b, 123–137.
13 Students admitted to universities and colleges from 1970 to 1976 were called "worker-peasant-soldier students" (工农兵学员), simply because they used to be workers, peasants and soldiers before being enrolled. During that period, this was the only access to higher education.
14 See the content of this letter and researchers' analyses of its significances in Liu 1998b, 376–382; and Gu 1997a, 129–134.
15 The eight major changes are explained in detail in Liu 1998b, 397–496.
16 See the detailed description of the Zhuzhou Model and the Leading Cadre System in Liu 1998b, 439–460.
17 Effective policies and measures like the Zhuzhou Model and the Leading Cadre System were disrupted. For details of the disturbance caused by the ultra-leftist faction, see Liu 1998b, 546–620.
18 In February 1976, Wu Guixian (吴桂贤), the vice-premier, sent a letter written by two Zhiqing in Shaanxi Province and her own letter to Mao Zedong, in which they expressed their concerns about the UMDC Movement. On 12 February, Mao wrote this brief comment on Wu's letter, which then became the new supreme instruction.
19 In September 1977, the Ministry of Education held the National Conference of Colleges and Universities Enrolment Work. On 21 October, the State Council announced the decision to resume the University/College Entrance Examination. According to the conference resolution, the entrance examination was open to workers, peasants, Zhiqing, veterans, cadres and new school graduates, and was guided by the principle of "unified examination, merit-based enrolment".
20 For further details on the conversations between central leaders and the petition group, see Gu 1997a, 187–192.
21 See more details about these measures in Gu 1997a, 198–204.
22 For details, see Gu 1997a, 211–216.
23 See Gu 1997a, 218–228; and Liu 1998b, 844–862, for further discussion of residual problems and solutions.
24 Thomas P. Bernstein published the first monograph on the UMDC Movement, *Up to the Mountains and Down to the Villages: The Transfer of Youth from Urban to Rural China*, in 1977. He is the originator of studies on the UMDC Movement in Western academia.
25 Rigorous historical study is beyond the scope of this study, but just to mention at least three questions that historians should consider: what costs would the state and society have paid to deal with the issue of urban surplus labour if there had been no "UMDC"?; how many of the 16 million urban youths would have received higher education if they had not gone to the countryside?; what would the rural economy and rural society have been like if the urbanization process had started in the 1960s?
26 In China, general statutory retirement ages are 60 for male executives and workers, 55 for female executives, and 50 for female workers.
27 From the 1970s, more opportunities to return to the city became available as UMDC policies loosened. Nevertheless, when Laosanjie managed to return to cities, they had been in the countryside for at least five years.
28 During the Cultural Revolution, a shortened nine-year schooling (Jiunian xuezhi 九年学制) was applied – that is, five years at primary school, two years at junior high school and two years at senior high school. The exact length of schooling

varied from province to province. Ten-year schooling was also seen in some parts of China, with some regions using a "5-3-2" model and others a "5-2-3" model.

29 In accordance with the qualitative paradigm chosen for this research, variables tracking and statistical analysis are not used in either discussions of each cohort or cross-cohort comparison.
30 According to Ding Yizhuang's opinion, the "17-year education" was a significant influence on the UMDC Movement and Zhiqing group, especially for Laosanjie. She analysed characteristics of the "17-year education" in detail in Ding 1998b, 429–430.
31 During the Cultural Revolution, elementary education shrank to five years. The specific length of junior high school and senior high school varied from province to province, but generally the length of secondary education reduced from six years to four or five years. See more details in Li 2002a, 84–89.
32 The entrance examination was open to workers, peasants, Zhiqing, veterans, cadres and fresh school graduates. The data collected by the research do not show the percentage of Zhiqing in the total number of examinees or Zhiqing's acceptance rate.
33 After being employed, some Zhiqing received on-the-job skills training and further education in their work units. A few Zhiqing attended television and radio lectures, correspondence courses or obtained professional qualification certificates to enhance their skills and levels of education. However, the general situation is that most Zhiqing were poorly educated.
34 From 1968 to 1970, a few Zhiqing were recruited every year but the quota was much lower and the selection was much more rigorous than the situation after 1971. Besides, for some individuals, going to the countryside was simply going through the motions. Through their family connections, they would stay in the countryside for a year or even less before they got job placement. Apart from these two special cases, annual job recruitment was the main access for the majority of Zhiqing.
35 From 1970s to 1980s, Zhiqing from city workers' families were able to fill their parents' positions according to the Displacement System (Dingti zhidu 顶替制度).
36 Younger Zhiqing who came subsequently were usually different in certain ways, so Zhiqing would usually form small communities more easily with those who went to the countryside in the same year. Besides, Zhiqing's relationships with their peers and those with younger Zhiqing were also different. For instance, Laosanjie would have been low-level cadres like production team leaders and thus would supervise Xinwujie's and Houwujie's work and living.

3 To the wider world
Group-identity configuration I (1967–81)

The abrupt termination of the UMDC Movement divided Zhiqing's identification process into two stages. In this chapter and the next, the two stages are investigated separately under two themes: "to the wider world" and "drops of water in the ocean", which generalize the characteristics of each stage. The two chapters aim to uncover individual Zhiqing's perceptions and feelings about their group membership under different social historical circumstances. Some 32 life stories collected by in-depth interviews are analysed based on social identity theory. Max Van Manen's (1990) thematic analysis is adopted as the analytical approach.

According to Van Manen, the ultimate objective of thematic analysis is to determine and explicate meanings of human beings' lived experiences. Meanings cannot be grasped in an all-inclusive manner. However, themes, which Van Manen defines as the structure of meaning, could point to, allude to and hint at various meanings of a lived experience. In the case of this study, "being a Zhiqing" is the lived experience in question. Like all human experiences, it is fragmented, multifarious ongoing and thus a fundamentally unapproachable phenomenon. As insiders' own representation of their experiences, interviewees' life stories bridge the phenomenon and the observer who otherwise would be a rejected outsider.

As Figure 3.1 shows, the first step of interpreting Zhiqing's lived experiences is to reduce and process the accessible data – Zhiqing's life stories – down to a manageable dimension and an organized form for further analysis. During step one (data reduction and processing), reading and cross-story comparison, frequently mentioned subjects are captured as key themes of these life stories, according to exhaustion and mutual-exclusivity principles. They are the constituents of meaning in Van Manen's sense. In step two, key themes are analysed in detail through combined thematic analysis and social identity analysis. Thematic analysis seeks to interpret textual and contextual meanings of these key themes in different life stories, while social identity analysis focuses on social psychological implications

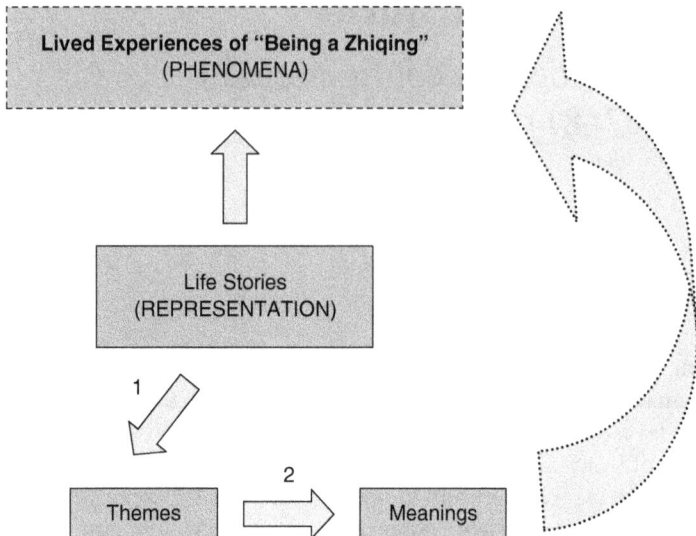

Figure 3.1 Processing and analysis of Zhiqing's life stories

of these themes – that is, storytellers' experiences, feelings and understandings of the Zhiqing group and their group membership.

3.1 Limited education

The majority of Zhiqing had only secondary or elementary education before they were sent to the countryside. Interviewees often complained about negative effects of their limited education on their later life. Interviewee 13 mocked the ironic name: "'Zhishi qingnian', so we were named. What kind of education did we have? Nonsense!" Nevertheless, some Zhiqing did continue their aspiration for knowledge in the countryside through self-teaching. Interviewee 1 recalled how they kept studying while doing heavy farm work:

> Most Zhiqing [had] just started [their] second year in junior high school. People like us only finished the first year in junior high school. [We] went to junior high school in 1965; the Cultural Revolution started in 1966. We didn't learn much. So [in the countryside] we simply did some reading and learning after working every day. At our place, people all knew that Zhiqing in this commune were very studious. Since 1972, seven to eight Zhiqing in our commune went to universities and colleges every year. Many of them were in the first batch of postgraduates and the first batch of overseas student with government sponsorship.

Self-study was often carried out in a collective way because Zhiqing were working and living together in a shared space. It was also one of the few recreational activities in the countryside. In some places, like interviewee 1's case, study was a spontaneous behaviour carried out by individuals or naturally formed study groups. Elsewhere it was done on a larger scale and was normally organized and regulated by corresponding authorities. Interviewee 14 went to a production and construction corps in Heilongjiang. He talked about the evening schools in his company:

> In our company, we set up an evening school to learn both knowledge and political documents. In the entire province, we were the first company to study philosophy. Journalists from the official newspaper of Heilongjiang Province came to interview us and later they made a whole-page report on philosophy study in our company. We studied not only politics but also other subjects like mathematics and literature. We offered different subjects in different classes. I noticed that people [showed] real initiative in studying. Teachers in the evening school were all selected from Zhiqing, and courses were open to anyone willing to come. The political slogan then was "Zhiqing should go to the countryside to get re-education from poor peasants". [I assumed that] there would be rare similar cases like our evening schools which encouraged and facilitated study in the countryside. However, when I went to work in the headquarters of our corps, I found that in fact there were similar study groups in every company.

Organized learning like evening schools provided better conditions and a stronger atmosphere than small-scale, spontaneous study groups. In his narration, interviewee 14 compared the advantages that corps had over production teams in terms of study:

> When we didn't need to work, at least 70–80 per cent [of] Zhiqing would be reading newspapers and books, and they would normally take notes. This was a very good atmosphere. Later especially, some people were consciously revising mathematics, physics and chemistry to get the opportunity for being recommended as worker-peasant-soldier students. Why was study in corps so highly valued? First, Zhiqing lived in a concentrated way. There were usually dozens or even hundreds [of] Zhiqing in one company. Some of them used to be classmates so they felt it was the same as school days. Besides, armies normally paid much attention to academic study. In such an environment, most Zhiqing were quite good at keeping on study. This was not the case for those who went to production teams. [O]n some occasions, there could be only one Zhiqing in one production team.

Many Zhiqing were motivated by practical reasons. Evidence of this is that self-study as a nationwide phenomenon did not appear until 1972 or 1973 when various opportunities, such as job recruitment, entry into colleges and universities and conscription, became available. To get selected, Zhiqing were supposed to demonstrate outstanding qualities, of which learning capacity was an element. No doubt that it was particularly important for those who sought higher education.

As a significant factor in life's opportunities, education level has a cumulative effect on an individual's socio-economic status and entire life path. Its influence on Zhiqing's life experiences was more obvious and profound in the post-UMDC era, partly because of the accumulation over time, but more importantly due to its association with a stereotype image of Zhiqing being poorly educated and incapable. Long-term effects of education and related social prejudice will be further elaborated in the next chapter.

3.2 The brief settling-in phase

Due to limited socio-economic conditions and ultra-leftist ideologies, Zhiqing were not given sufficient time to familiarize themselves with their new environment. In a very brief settling-in phase, these urban youth had to adapt to the different environment, lifestyle and culture in the countryside. Interviewees' narration shows that their first impressions of rural life and rural society varied in many ways. Some were relatively young when they moved to the countryside. As interviewee 12 said, they were too ignorant to understand what the new life would mean:

> I was small at that time; we barely knew anything [laugh]. Well, I just felt it was quite fresh. We were simply muddleheaded teenagers, having no idea about the future or anything, just knowing to work hard and earn work points. Seriously, I thought about nothing and I knew nothing.

By contrast, interviewee 5 had a more sophisticated notion of the upcoming new life:

> As an urban kid who just went to the countryside, I noticed that some significant and complex changes were happening in my mind. At first, everything was so fresh. Going to the village was just like dropping round. Then one morning, I woke up early at about 5:30am and I saw that peasants had come back for breakfast from the field after early work, and they would soon leave to work again after breakfast. I was so shocked and I realized that I was no longer an urban child; I was a real peasant now.

Apart from this relatively rational reaction, a combined feeling of sadness and hopelessness is another common emotion in interviewees' life stories. For example, interviewee 15 said:

> After two days and three nights on the train, it took another whole night on a big truck to get to the place. In that darkness, I couldn't see anything, and I didn't know how far the truck had gone. I thought perhaps I could never come back. I simply didn't know how I could get out of such a desolate place. It cooled my ardour.

Production and construction corps (生产建设兵团) and collective farms were better in terms of infrastructure and living conditions. Zhiqing in these places had different attitudes and perceptions from the abovementioned examples. Interviewee 13 said that he was quite surprised to see that the conditions were much better than he had imagined:

> Our impression of the Great Northern Wilderness [Beidahuang 北大荒] was: Oh! It must be quite desolate. It should be further cultivated. When I got there, I saw that every family lived in a brick house with [an] electricity supply. Besides, agriculture work was mechanized. We had prepared to live a harsh life, yet on seeing these conditions, we thought: was it real? This was good!

The situation in corps and farms was relatively better but still worse than that in the city. Every Zhiqing, no matter where they went, had to cope with an intensive work schedule, geographic and cultural changes, and different living habits. On the other hand, things they experienced as strange and challenging were daily routines for generations of local villagers. In other words, it was these "unusual" things and uncomfortable feelings that highlighted the distinction between Zhiqing and their surroundings. According to social identity theory, both the group formation and individual's self-identification are activated by the perceived intergroup differences. The ingroup-outgroup meta-contrast is primarily a formal differentiation. The above quotations show that the Zhiqing-peasant formal differentiation became concrete and relevant to individual Zhiqing through practical problems with which they were confronted on a day-to-day basis. Therefore, based on Zhiqing's life stories and social identity theory, it is reasonable to infer that:

1   the settling-in phase marked the beginning of the formation of the Zhiqing group and the group membership (i.e. the Zhiqing identity), by providing a material basis for these two processes;

2   the existence of the Zhiqing group would become perceivable and relevant to individuals only when they personally experienced differences between their own group and a contrasting group, namely peasants (during the UMDC Movement) and urban citizens (in the post-UMDC era);
3   similarly, an individual would not fully realize the salience of his/her group membership (the Zhiqing identity), until he/she encountered members from other social groups or other intergroup circumstances.

To be more specific, what mattered directly to individual Zhiqing was not official documentation or abstract ideology but concrete life details as well as their experience and understanding of these details. Zhiqing's later experience of resettlement in the city proved again that the salience of group membership is activated by the recognition of a boundary between groups, even though the contrasting group and the socio-historical environment both altered at that time.

3.3 Blend into the rural society

The ultimate goal of the UMDC Movement was to transform those urban youth into real peasants. In practice, relocation of Zhiqing in the countryside was supposed to be permanent, until new policies were implemented in 1972 and 1973. Nevertheless, every year the quota for each production team (or corps or farm) was quite limited and the selection criterion was that each candidate must have performed their peasant role with assiduity for at least two years. In a word, willingly or reluctantly, Zhiqing had to blend in and become part of the rural society. Compared with the settling-in phase, this was a much longer and tougher journey. As shown in interviewees' life stories, the related experience was composed of two themes: farm work and the Zhiqing-peasant relationship.

3.3.1 Farm work

Many interviewees took time to describe details of farm work and other manual labour they did in the countryside. General plots and their implied meanings were largely identical: they worked extremely hard and suffered too much from the heavy work. Managing farm work was a basic priority and simple task for each peasant. Yet as urban youth, most Zhiqing struggled greatly to meet this criterion. Farm work was a main part of Zhiqing's rural life. From a theoretical perspective, several implications of this everyday routine can be identified.

First, farm work was not simply a daily event, but also a field where ingroup and intergroup relationships took shape. On one hand, interviewees often refer to their experiences of collective work to justify why connections they built in the countryside are still maintained today. They use obvious causal conjunctions like "because" – "because we had endured hardships together" – or metaphors like "we were just like comrades-in-arms in the same trench", to illustrate the profound friendship that they established through collective farm work. This indicates that task interdependence was an influential factor for the formation and solidarity of the Zhiqing group. On the other hand, farm work further concretized and intensified the Zhiqing-peasant formal differentiation, and thereby contributed to the formation of the Zhiqing group and the salience of the Zhiqing identity.

Second, farm work also facilitated Zhiqing's identification process by propelling the RII mechanism.[1] It brings into being certain group prototypes which initiated the depersonalization of originally diversified individuals. For instance, working hard is acknowledged as Zhiqing's general character which, in interviewees' narration, is associated with heavy farm work. Interviewee 1's story offers a good example.

> Generally, Zhiqing in our village were very tough. Sometimes, we even frightened local villagers. Once we were mending a river embankment. One Zhiqing shouted out loud and then male and female Zhiqing all jumped into the river to stop the running water. It was winter time and the river was freezing. Seeing this, villagers exerted to their utmost to fill and tamp, and eventually we blocked the hole. Only Zhiqing dared to do this and work so hard.

According to social identity theory, the progression from "settling in" to "blending in" in fact illustrated the functioning of the RII in real life:

1 in the settling-in phase, individuals acquired their categorical membership (the Zhiqing identity) by recognizing the Zhiqing-peasant formal differentiation;
2 in the blending-in phase, individual Zhiqing ascertained that certain ways of behaving were appropriate, expected or desired attributes of the category membership. These attributes included mastering farm work skills, working hard and enduring hardship;
3 also in the blending-in phase, individual Zhiqing assigned these norms to themselves in the same way as they assign other stereotypic characteristics of the category to themselves when their category membership becomes psychologically salient. Thus their behaviour became more normative (conformist) as their category membership became salient.

In the original theory of RII, members would ascertain attributes of their category membership to define it as different from other categories.[2]

For Zhiqing, however, stereotypes and prototypes did not differentiate Zhiqing from the contrasting group – peasants – but identified them with it. This confusing fact leads to the next theme: the Zhiqing-peasant relationship.

3.3.2 The Zhiqing-peasant relationship

The RII mechanism is summarized based on minimal group experiments in which intergroup relations are simplified and influences from sociohistorical factors are minimized. Group processes in the real world are much more complicated. A telos of the UMDC Movement was to find solutions to the entrenched rural-urban dual structure, by relocating urban youth to the countryside and transforming them into real peasants. In practice, however, the Zhiqing group was incorporated into the binary system. More importantly, the ideal scenario of definite categorization turned out to be a grey zone where the Zhiqing group was exposed to the tension between the countryside (peasants) and the city (urban citizens), and hence received influences from both extremes.

Historical facts suggest that: 1 the Zhiqing group was fundamentally alien to both sides but it could be temporarily assimilated with one side depending upon its exact position at a particular time; and 2 its position wandered back and forth in the binary system, driven by the changing relation of the two powers. The grey zone has the following implications for Zhiqing's individuals' perception of the group and their identification behaviours:

1 due to the effect of temporal assimilation, certain attributes from both extremes were ascertained as prototypes of the Zhiqing group, which means they both have latent effects on the Zhiqing group;
2 different circumstances would activate different prototypes and identification behaviours – for instance, once an extreme group is regarded as an outgroup, prototypes drawn from the other extreme group would become salient;
3 due to the effect of social categorization, Zhiqing may be perceived as homogeneous with one extreme group by the other, yet Zhiqing themselves could never fully identify with either of the two groups.

Tajfel's Law is applicable here to explain Zhiqing's identification with the peasant group. During the UMDC Movement, Zhiqing and peasants were categorized by the same "rural" membership which would minimize their differences and lead to ingroup homogeneity. In addition, the grey zone reveals the essence of Zhiqing's confused sense of belonging – the absolute alienation in the binary system resulted for social, historical and cultural reasons. This feeling of confusion and alienation gave rise to particular features of Zhiqing's identification attitudes and behaviours which will be analysed later in relevant themes. A key feature of the Zhiqing-peasant relationship is the variety and ambivalence of Zhiqing's attitudes towards peasants and rural society. Interviewee 1 spoke frankly about her gratitude to villagers: "Many villagers were really kind-hearted. They knew that we were underfed, and they usually bought us some food when they cooked something nice." This notion of a harmonious relationship suggests the interviewee's appreciation of unsophisticated villagers as well as the plain ethics and culture of rural society. Conflicts were simply inevitable but Zhiqing's feelings and interpretations of their conflict with peasants are complicated. This can be seen in interviewee 20's narration:

> To be honest, Mao Zedong said the poor and lower-middle peasants should welcome Zhiqing. What's the meaning of this? It means that Zhiqing were not welcomed by peasants. Why? Their lives were very difficult. When we were eating steamed rice, those kids watched us so eagerly. Poor kids. Since we came to the countryside, they had to share their food with us. How could they be willing to do so? Although they are kind-hearted, and they dared not question government policies, they basically didn't understand [the policy]. Conflicts? Not necessarily. Why? You know, peasants there were very simple, some are extremely kind-hearted. They would love to help you, even though their situations were awful, they would like to help you.

At a deeper level, Zhiqing's worldview and values gradually changed while they were living in the rural society. Many Zhiqing began to question political discourses and dominant ideologies. For example, interviewee 4 recalled her doubts on the re-education theory:

> Talking about re-education by the poor and lower-middle peasants, sometimes peasants' educational levels vary so much . . . I wondered with such a quality, how could we get his education? We laughed at him privately. However, we were at [a] loss while laughing, wouldn't you say so? It was just this kind of feeling. They did teach us how to do farm work though. We learnt each procedure from tilling to harvest.

Many interviewees also believed that Zhiqing and peasants both gained certain positive outcomes. On one hand, Zhiqing learned from peasants and acquired some good features like working hard and integrity; on the other hand, Zhiqing brought in the urban culture which local villagers had not had the chance to observe. As interviewee 14 said:

You know, the countryside has changed a lot. This would never happen if Zhiqing didn't go there. Originally, they didn't know about brushing their teeth or using tissue paper . . . Zhiqing were just like a link between the city and the countryside . . . Consequently, most peasants flock to urban areas nowadays. They know that surely it's better to move to the city than staying in the countryside. How come this didn't happen before? Of course they didn't have the opportunity to travel, but it was also because they used to be so ill-informed. Now that they know there is another world, of course they would like to see it and to pursue it.

The above quotations demonstrate Zhiqing's complex attitudes towards peasants and rural society, which as explained earlier could be attributed to the grey zone and their feelings of confusion and alienation. Moreover, it seems that in collected life stories, narrators deliberately left their attitudes and perceptions unclarified. According to Turner's motivational explanation, this deliberate ambiguity could be seen as a special strategy for securing the positive distinctiveness of the Zhiqing group under the circumstance of uncertainties in the grey zone, including the indefinite ingroup-outgroup boundary, the coexistence of prototypes from two opposing groups and the changing power relations. Chapter 4 will return to the topic of positive distinctiveness and discuss Zhiqing's complex identification attitudes in the post-UMDC era.

Apart from its identification-related significance, the Zhiqing-peasant relationship also forms an important part of Zhiqing's interrelated lives. From the above-quoted narrations it can be seen that experiences in the countryside widened Zhiqing's interrelated lives, which resulted in external changes (e.g. widened interpersonal networks and experiences of geographical and cultural diversity), as well as underlying transformations of their living habits, ways of thinking, behaviour patterns and personal character. Effects of these external and internal changes on Zhiqing's later life will be further discussed in Chapter 4.

3.4 Zhiqing's collective life and activities

Like the farm work, Zhiqing's collective life was another important field where ingroup and intergroup relationships, formation of the Zhiqing group and individual Zhiqing's self-identification took place.

The content and nature of Zhiqing's collective lives varied according to where they lived. For those who were sent to production teams, collectivity to them normally refers to the household they shared with a few others, just as interviewee 1 summarized: "We lived like a family, a sort of collective household." For those in corps and farms, the scope of their collectivity is much larger. Besides, activities in corps and farms were more frequent and more diversified because of better facilities and stronger administration. In production teams, collective activities were normally self-organized and self-dependent, as interviewee 3 explained:

> The head of the collective household managed it. We elected a head, a committeeman of life and a committeeman of labour. [The] committeeman of labour took care of farm work, [the] committeeman of life took charge of daily necessaries and the head did the general management.

While Zhiqing in corps and farms were strictly organized by a hierarchy of authorities, Zhiqing in production teams were largely accountable for their own livelihood, in terms of collective activities and everyday life in general. This means that qualities of collective life in different households may vary – a phenomenon that interviewee 9 attributed to individuals' efforts:

> We set up a flagpole in front of our house, and we had our own flag-raising ceremony. Collective activities were contingent on how well you steered them. We didn't sing the national song. Raising a flag simply meant to demonstrate that we were one household, we were a collective. That was what it meant . . . It depended on how you organized. If you organized it well, it would have positive influences on the society and the village, but if not, it would have negative effects. It depended on human efforts, which itself depended on people in the collective, their qualities and whether they were held together or not . . . It depended on how you organize. Steering and direction was very important. It relied on your own efforts.

Comparatively, collective life of the Zhiqing in corps and farms was more secured and standardized. Its downsides were the stringent regulation and rigid supervision. A typical example was compulsory study of political documents.[3] Interviewee 13 described the resistance that most Zhiqing had towards this obligatory activity:

> We asked for instructions every morning and reported every evening [zao qingshi, wan huibao 早请示:晚汇报]. Alas! It was really dizzy and giddy. In fact, we were all sick of the affair and disgusted with it. Young people would love to stay in bed early morning. However, we had to get up at 5am. Our team leader wouldn't stop knocking on the door until we got up. After breakfast, we had to read for an hour every day; I didn't really pay attention to what I was reading. In the evening, we had to listen to the news on China National Radio until the programme ended

at 8.30pm; and after that there was usually a meeting, repeating the same cliché. You couldn't get to bed until 9pm or 10pm. At that time, we only slept for [a] few hours a day. This was what I hated the most.

The above narrations illustrate that through collective activities, certain conventions and norms were established and acquired by Zhiqing. Since these conventions and norms, such as living and working together as independent small collectives, were specific to Zhiqing, they distinguished the Zhiqing group from its contrast groups, namely local villagers, military officers and farm workers. On a deeper layer, conventions and norms were also perceived and practised by individual Zhiqing as cognitive and behavioural rules. When conventions and norms became stabilized as part of everyday life and internalized by individuals, they gradually solidified and evolved into group prototypes which then would be taught to new members. In this way, Zhiqing's collective life in fact exemplifies the functioning of the RII mechanism.

Interviewee 13's words quoted above reveal that individuals' minds were not simply the reflection of group conventions and norms. In fact, many Zhiqing had doubts and discontent and sometimes even violated the norms. Nevertheless, in their life stories, they still expressed a strong sense of togetherness and belonging to the collective. This could be explained by Murray Horwitz and Jacob M. Rabbie's notion of group formation and group cohesiveness. Horwitz and Rabbie (1982, 241–277) argue that group formation is initiated by the perceived interdependence among individuals, and that group cohesiveness is generated by individual members' task interdependence and interdependence of fate. In the above quotations, interviewee 3 and interviewee 9 illustrated, respectively, Zhiqing's behavioural conformity in acting on a group task as their mutual goal (task interdependence) and a sense of being responsible for the welfare of their household (interdependence of fate).

Theorists disagree as to the primary cause of group formation and group cohesiveness.[4] Zhiqing's life stories state clearly that social force and individualist efforts both played an important role in the formation of the Zhiqing group, and that cohesiveness of the Zhiqing group had both affective (emotional ties) and instrumental (behavioural conformity) outcomes. This shows that social comparison and interdependence are not necessarily conflicting and in fact could not be separated. Zhiqing in production teams where social forces were relatively weak were influenced by the same social norms, while those in corps and farms were well able to form interdependence with their ingroup members.

Although Zhiqing had little time for recreational activities due to the intensive work schedule all year round, they managed to find several ways to enjoy themselves. This was described by them as "seeing joy amidst sorrow". In a proud and delighted tone, interviewee 3 talked about how they managed to have some fun with limited resources:

> Even in those tough days, we were very happy and cheerful. By the end of a day, we gathered in our house – boys would play instruments and girls would sing. From far away, some local villagers would be attracted by us. Girls love beauty and we were quite trendy even at that time. Sometimes we made a special hairstyle, the next day, young village girls would imitate us. We would change to another style when we noticed that, then they would imitate us again. It was like we were leading the trend.

On certain occasions, for example National Day and Chinese New Year, there would be large-scale celebratory activities. Watching a movie was one of these big events. Interviewee 17 was a film projectionist. He recalled this experience:

> Collective activities, well, I had a best advantage. I was welcomed every place I went to, because showing a movie provided everyone [with] an opportunity to get together. Some Zhiqing would run over ten miles to see a movie. Some would follow me from one production team to another just to see movies. At that time, seeing movies was one of the biggest collective activities. Apart from that, there would be New Year performances organized by each commune. We were so lacking in cultural activities that showing a movie would be the most bustling time.

In the course of the UMDC Movement, Zhiqing's collective life also changed over time. Changes to the political situation as well as adjustments in the UMDC Movement policies had significant impacts on the Zhiqing group, causing instabilities to Zhiqing's collective life. Interviewee 16 went to a national farm in Yunnan and stayed there for ten years. He witnessed changes of Zhiqing's collective life throughout the decade: "At the beginning, it was military-style management, but later it was impossible to manage. [This was] because of instabilities." Interviewee 17's experience explains where these instabilities came from:

> The most unstable time was 1972 and 1973 when some Zhiqing started to leave through conscription and university enrolment. At that time, the collective life went wobbly under such impact. At the beginning, things were very simple. Even though some of us were promoted as leaders, we were all stable emotionally. When you saw others leave,

you would think about yourself. How would this end for you? You didn't know. That was the most painful moment. Labour work was very hard undoubtedly; you had to do it if you wanted to live. But when you saw someone leaving, you would wonder: where would my destiny to be? . . . I think the greatest impact on the Zhiqing community was the personnel transfer. Once this opening was made, [the] following impacts were significant. Of course, we had never expected that Zhiqing would all return to the city in 1978. No one had foreseen that.

Obviously, at a later stage of the UMDC Movement, external socio-historical changes such as policy adjustments shook the foundations of the Zhiqing group by threatening established group norms and individuals' interdependence, and thus caused group members' perception of internal instabilities.

To summarize: from the settling-in phase to the blending-in phase, certain prototypes of the Zhiqing group gradually formed and consolidated group membership. The Zhiqing identity was also taking shape in the meantime. On this foundation, Zhiqing's collective life further intensified the depersonalization by activating the contextual shift from individualist mode to group mode, and thereby "switched on" the group mode of each individual's self-concept. While the depersonalization went on, another simultaneous process – group-identity configuration – also progressed. Group norms and individuals' interdependence were constructed through collective activities, which propelled the group-identity configuration on both instrumental and affective levels.

3.5 Zhiqing's personal relationships

Chapter 2 mentioned briefly that Zhiqing's interrelated lives were enriched by the expanded interpersonal network that they established during the UMDC Movement. It took time to build harmonious relations. Reasons were very simple and practical, as interviewee 1 explained:

> After we settled in the village, you see, a bunch of kids in an unfamiliar environment, whether we managed to take care of ourselves and so on, [all could be problems]. [Life was] very hard, and lots of conflicts arose. Primarily, food was not enough, we were underfed. [This] caused many conflicts . . . You see, a flock of kids from different families came to live together; how could we have no conflict? We had various family backgrounds, right? Definitely there would be quarrels.

As they spent more time together, Zhiqing in the same collective gradually established affection for and commitment to each other. In the meantime the group-identity configuration was also taking place which in turn impacted on Zhiqing's cognition and behaviour. This dialectical process gave rise to close personal relationships in the Zhiqing group, which they described as "brotherhood" and "sisterhood", as interviewee 6 recalled:

> We are all from the city. Boys and girls took care of each other. Boys would help girls to carry water and girls would help boys to wash clothes. But at that age, we were very innocent, we never thought about dating or getting together. We were just like brothers and sisters.

Most Zhiqing, such as interviewee 6, believed in Zhiqing's genuine friendship and suggested that this quasi-kinship relationship was superior to other types of social relationships:

> These Zhiqing lived together for five or six years, are truly lifelong friends. Some said Zhiqing were even closer than their sisters. You could count on them when you have troubles. You might not speak to each other for three or five months but once you have a problem, he/she will try his/her best [to help]. This is it.

As was discussed in the last section, Horwitz and Rabbie (1982), and Tajfel and Turner (Tajfel 1982) offered two models to explain group cohesiveness: the attraction-based cohesion which results in group solidarity (affective outcome); and the commitment-based cohesion which leads to group members' homogeneity in thoughts and behaviour (instrumental outcome). Again, Zhiqing's life experiences testify that interpersonal attraction and ingroup commitment as two origins of group cohesiveness coexist in the group formation process, and that both forces were significant to the maintenance of the Zhiqing group in different ways.

For example, in interviewee 1's story, when she talked about Zhiqing's friendship in general, she referred to the length of time they had spent together: "these Zhiqing, like us who lived together for five or six years, are truly lifelong friends, friends for life." Later when she talked about Zhiqing's marriage, she referred to common topics and similar mindset: "many people tend to find Zhiqing as their spouse, because of the same experience, the common language." Apparently, by spending that length of time together, individuals could form ingroup commitment and emotional ties as well. Interviewee 1's narration focused on her personal network. Hence she talked about cohesiveness mainly in the context of emotional ties based on personal interactions. Other interviewees narrated encounters with other Zhiqing whom they had never met before. They described the situation that both parties immediately felt a sense of affinity which they seldom had while interacting with other people. In fact, this "encounter" plot is quite common in interviewees' life stories, which suggests that in large groups like the Zhiqing, cohesiveness is not generated solely by interpersonal affective relations or individuals' common attributes, but also by ingroup commitment which derives from individual members' identification with the group membership and their compliance with group prototypes. After the end of the UMDC Movement, Zhiqing became socially stratified and emotionally alienated. What gives them the sense of affinity in those random encounters is not personal affection but the shared Zhiqing identity. To be more specific: I recognize my membership of the Zhiqing group so I feel a sense of belongingness and togetherness with other members, rather than the other way around.

To summarize, within one's personal networks, members experience and re-intensify the attraction-based group cohesion, while in the entire Zhiqing group, members are bound by a commitment-based cohesion formed and maintained by structural forces. In the last few years, Zhiqing's collective activities have become more frequent. Zhiqing from different provinces would get together and organize tourist trips. In these circumstances, it is the commitment-based cohesion that provides the basis for them to rebuild lost connections and develop new friendships. Within a smaller scope, a specific Zhiqing association for instance, there could be subgroups made up of several individuals who feel closer to each other because of their similar experience or personality. The next chapter will discuss the topic of Zhiqing's personal relationship again by focusing on its new features that formed in the post-UMDC era.

Zhiqing's various attitudes towards their personal relationships is another issue worth studying. While talking enthusiastically about their life-long friendship, interviewee 1 admitted: "There are also Zhiqing who never contact or have been out of touch for many reasons. Besides, there are Zhiqing who are not so close to each other." Interviewee 5 has a clear understanding of Zhiqing's divergent perceptions of the group and their mutual relations:

> We were from different schools and we didn't know each other before moving to the village. At first, it was harmonious. Over time, conflicts started to arise. In those three years, it would take at least one year for us to know each other, and then the basic structure took shape, that was everyone's position in this group. It was just like any other group. [We] acted towards the outside out of a pretty strong centripetal force; nevertheless, we had intrigues, fights and quarrels inside the collective household as well. It's a natural phenomenon among human beings. Why was it called a collective household? It was family-like. It was quite natural but also abstract: natural because human lives are all the same; abstract because we seemed like a family but actually we were not a family in the real sense. Everybody had his/her own thoughts and

routines, yet anyhow you felt like one family consciously or subconsciously. That was how you were positioned.

Interviewee 5 pointed out the underlying contradiction between the ambiguous "family-like" nature of the collective household and the undoubtable result of social categorization: "That was how you were positioned." Interviewee 5's awareness of both sides of the contradiction and Zhiqing's divergent attitudes illustrate that depersonalization is not a once and for all process, nor would it replace unique individuality with group prototypes. As clarified in social identity theory, group prototypes, categorical membership and the depersonalized self are all contextually salient. They come into force only in social comparison circumstances, as simple as interviewee 5 said: "[We] acted towards the outside out of a pretty strong centripetal force; nevertheless, we had intrigues, fights and quarrels inside the collective household as well." In addition to this, the contradiction and divergent attitudes also state clearly that the attraction-resulted group solidarity and the commitment-resulted group conformity are two distinct phenomena which have no correlative or causal relation, and therefore they should always be understood separately in their respective contexts.

3.6 Visit home in the city

According to relevant policies, Zhiqing were allowed to have short vacations to visit relatives in the city once every year or every other year. The length of the vacation was usually about two weeks. Besides the short duration, there were other obstacles for fully enjoying them. Distance was a major problem, as interviewee 14 said:

> I visited Shanghai in the third year. We were allowed to stay for a fortnight. In these two weeks, I would spend three days and four nights on the road. Think about it. I took vacations for at most five times. We were allowed to visit home every year. Because the distance was too far, we visited home every two years.

Another concern was the cost for their families. Some Zhiqing chose to stay in the countryside even at Chinese New Year just because they did not have the money for travel. Interviewee 3 recalled her experience, which was in fact a common situation in China then:

> Our families were usually short of food at that time. Your supply had been reallocated to the countryside. Each urban resident had 27.5 jin[5] of grain every month. You would be eating others' food when you stayed

in your home. So normally I wouldn't go home. Sometimes my siblings wouldn't be very happy either. At that time, our country was under difficult conditions, [we] had no money.

On the other hand, Zhiqing also benefited from visiting their relatives in the city. On each vacation, Zhiqing would receive certain material and financial aid from their families to cover their lives in the countryside. Many interviewees talked about getting pocket money from their parents, and bringing pork, noodles, oil and other resources back to share with each other.

More importantly, these short vacations triggered Zhiqing's complicated feelings. Some interviewees mentioned the strangeness they felt on their first vacation after about two or three years in the countryside. As illustrated by interviewee 15, they had become unaccustomed to things:

> Well, I felt that Shanghai was pretty small [since] I had lived in the bigger world. Oh, how come these streets were so narrow? In Heilongjiang, it was quite broad everywhere. Having stayed in the countryside for three years, I felt streets in Shanghai appeared narrow. Anyway, I found everything sort of strange. This was really the most immediate feeling. Then I felt streets were packed and noisy, I didn't like it.

Interviewee 13's narration was more emotional:

> On these vacations, I always had this inferiority complex. I felt that I was an outsider, not belonging to this city. During the UMDC Movement, on my vacations I always felt apart from the whole city. I felt that I was a stranger to the city and I never thought about any connections between it and myself. It was just because my parents were here and I wanted to visit my family and enjoy the hard-earned 12-day holiday every year. Besides, I could eat something nice if I wished to and bring some good stuff back. [I was] simply a stranger of the city. After I returned [to the city eventually], well, I was a member of the city again, so everything mattered to me again. Before that, this hadn't been the case. What did anything in this city have to do with me? I wouldn't care about what was happening in this city.

This "inferiority complex" could be attributed to the huge rural–urban gap which became evident and relevant to Zhiqing during their short stay in the city. Interviewee 16's bittersweet story of eating wonton illustrated Zhiqing's perceptions of these two different worlds:

> Do you know the first thing after we got off the old railway station in Shanghai? We would rush out of the station to the wonton shop

across the street. Normally we wouldn't have eaten these things for two or four years. Other customers there were so shocked on seeing the way we ate wonton. They normally ate one or two [cage drawers of wonton], and that would be a lot for them. When we were eating there, those cage drawers would pile up very high. You could imagine how hard the life was in the countryside. They were simply two completely different worlds.

Like undercurrents, the above listed and other complicated emotions and ideas triggered by short vacations gradually accumulated. When related policies were introduced to offer Zhiqing opportunities to return to the city, these emotions and ideas finally found an outlet, and together with the policies, they caused instabilities to the Zhiqing group as described by interviewee 17: "When you saw others leave, you would think about yourself ... That was the most painful moment." Interviewee 28 talked of the anger she felt on her last vacation because of her anxiety about her unsettled future:

During the time of my last vacation, I felt so irritable. I fought with my dad all the time. Because I had no job, nothing. Thinking about it now, I [have figured out that] it was simply because I was still in the countryside with very little salary and my future was still unsettled. What should I do?

Interviewee 28's narration shows that underneath her irrational anger there were deeper feelings of hopelessness, helplessness and anxiety. Another kind of negative emotion, as represented in interviewee 29's narration, was a sense of shame and humiliation:

I only took three times of vacations. There was nothing special at the first time. At the second time, I noticed others' judging eyes, or maybe I was too sensitive. My younger sister had started working at that time. She bought me a scarf. I just hated that I still had to use her money. I got only 40 yuan RMB. After spending money on my tickets, I didn't do much shopping in Shanghai. I was reluctant to spend the 40 yuan RMB which I had taken huge efforts to earn. I didn't feel like going home at the third time but my dad missed me so much. That was really hard for me, really hard. When I knew I could come back to Shanghai to study in a university, I kept that confidential. I decided that I wouldn't tell them until I eventually got enrolled. So when I finally returned to Shanghai, I went to my classmate's home to have a bath; I cleaned up myself and then came home. They thought I was on a vacation. I told them I probably had been admitted by the Sports College.

58 *To the wider world*

Compared with the above two interviewees, interviewee 27 was in a better situation because she had been promoted as a cadre before she took her first vacation. However, she also had inner struggles about her embarrassing position because the promotion prohibited her from seeking opportunities to return to the city. Her experience indicates how significant returning to the city was for every Zhiqing.

> On my first vacation, because I had been promoted and I had joined the Party, surely my dad and mum were proud of me. I was invited to give a speech for a new batch of Zhiqing at my school. I behaved quite actively at that time, so I didn't mention much about those difficulties . . . I was still in a mood of lofty sentiment at the first time because I [had] just joined the Party. Then gradually, as you stayed longer, you would begin to admire [urban residents] after all. They lived in the city; I would end up in this poor remote area. However, you couldn't search for opportunities to return to cities like other Zhiqing did because you had declared your standpoint of taking root in the village and you were a cadre. There were many people watching you.

The most obvious impact of these short vacations was Zhiqing's emotional reactions. More crucially, vacations in the city highlighted the intergroup difference between Zhiqing (countryside) and urban citizens (city). Thus it perturbed conventions and norms of Zhiqing's lives and essentially disrupted the functioning of the Zhiqing group, its cohesiveness and individuals' identification. According to the analysis of the grey zone above, the external influence from these vacations intensified the tension between the peasants group and the urban citizens group, gave rise to Zhiqing's confusion about different prototypes ascertained from the two sides and resulted in their inner struggles. In a fundamental sense, the above-listed forms of negative emotions all pointed to a feeling of relative deprivation, as interviewee 27 summarized: "They lived in the city. I would end up in this poor remote area." Relative deprivation is related to many key themes of Zhiqing's lives in the post-movement era – for instance, resettling experiences, personal relationships in the city and contacts with the countryside. While analysing these themes in the latter half of interviewees' life stories, Chapter 4 will further elaborate implications of the relative deprivation and Zhiqing's coping strategies.

3.7 Summary

This chapter examined Zhiqing's lives during the UMDC Movement when they were categorized as a new group and were sent out from their home cities to settle down in "the wider world". As the first half of the group-identity configuration, this was the stage when the formation and functioning of the Zhiqing group, the group cohesiveness and the Zhiqing identity took place. Analysis of the first theme, Zhiqing's low education level, touched upon impacts of education on Zhiqing's life chances during the UMDC period. As suggested in that section, such a disadvantage affected Zhiqing's opportunities in life much more significantly in the post-UMDC era. Chapter 4 will continue this discussion by taking into consideration related stereotypes of Zhiqing as well as its socio-cultural origins.

Subsequent sections of this chapter constitute a comprehensive description of the formation and function of the Zhiqing group, its cohesion and its membership – the Zhiqing identity. By combining thematic analysis and social identity theory, the chapter elaborated important theoretical issues based on details of interviewees' narrations – namely, initiation of the group-forming process, concretization of the ingroup-outgroup meta-contrast, formation and solidification of group prototypes, depersonalization of individual members, and the origins and effects of group cohesion. Those life details offer a way to understand how the group-identity configuration was experienced, perceived and internalized by individual Zhiqing themselves.

The last section explained how vacations in cities had destabilized established outcomes of the group-identity configuration on the cognitive level before political, social and economic changes could actually take place. Those external changes, however, had direct and decisive influences on the fortune of the Zhiqing group, and thus led to specific characteristics of the second half of the group-identity configuration and resulted in Zhiqing's current status – "drops of water in the ocean".

Notes

1 See details about RII in section 1.2.3 of Chapter 1.
2 Ibid.
3 In fact, the study of political documents was a compulsory requirement for Zhiqing in production teams as well, but the enforcement in corps and farms were much stricter.
4 See Horwitz and Rabbie 1982.
5 Jin (斤) is a Chinese unit of measurement. One jin is equal to 500 grams.

4 Drops of water in the ocean
Group-identity configuration II (1980s–present)

The life course analysis in Chapter 2 shows that returning to the city was a critical life transition that fundamentally changed Zhiqing's identification process and behaviours. This chapter will first explain the relevant historical context of this critical event and then explain its significant influences on Zhiqing's life in the post-movement era.

4.1 The critical transition: Zhiqing's massive retreat and hasty resettlement

After Mao Zedong's death in 1976, the future of the UMDC Movement became ambiguous due to political uncertainties. At the Second National Conference of the UMDC Work, at the end of 1978, the central leadership reached a consensus that the movement should carry on for the foreseeable future, and that policy adjustments had to be made to improve Zhiqing's living conditions in the countryside. Viewing this conference as a signal of power change in the central leadership, a few leaders in the Zhiqing group decided to take this advantage to make their appeal.

Demonstrations, strikes and other forms of protest broke out in Yunnan and Heilongjiang and quickly spread all over the country at the end of 1978. In response, the State Council sent an investigation team to Yunnan to gather information about Zhiqing's protests and their requirements in December 1978. Based on the report by this investigation team, the state released informal permission for Zhiqing to return to their home cities in early 1979. In less than two years (1978–79), over 6 million Zhiqing rushed back to their home cities (see Table 4.1). This was known as Zhiqing's Massive Retreat. The termination of the UMDC Movement was officially announced in 1980.[1]

As Table 4.1 shows, in 1978, over 2.5 million Zhiqing returned to the city, which was over five times the number of Zhiqing who went to the countryside in the same year. The year 1978 was also the key year when the number of Zhiqing in the countryside started to decrease. Table 4.2 gives detailed figures of Zhiqing who returned to the city through different channels before and

Table 4.1 Scale of the UMDC Movement (1976–79)

Year	Zhiqing sent down	Zhiqing returned to the city	Zhiqing in the countryside
1976	1,880,000	1,350,000	7,950,000
1977	1,710,000	1,030,000	8,640,000
1978	480,000	2,550,000	6,570,000
1979	240,000	3,950,000	2,860,000

Source: From Liu 1998b; and Bonnin 2009; reproduced with permission from Chinese University Press

during the Massive Retreat. These figures and their year-on-year variations reflect complex situations during the transitional period from 1976 to 1978.

"Other" in the last column referred mainly to two special situations: leaving the countryside because of illness or family difficulties, and filling parents' job positions in the city. These were the two main channels for those who failed in fierce competition for job recruitment, university admission and conscription. As a matter of fact, many Zhiqing cheated in physical examinations or even injured themselves to get the illness certification. Many parents chose early retirement to get their children back to fill their positions. Conscription and higher education led to better career prospects and higher social status. Competition for these opportunities was much fiercer. The state recruited 298,100 soldiers from Zhiqing in 1978, which was the highest number in the four years from 1976 to 1979. During the UMDC Movement, around 1 million Zhiqing entered universities and colleges, including worker-peasant-soldier students.[2] This means that only 6.2 per cent of the 16 million Zhiqing received tertiary-level education and thus had a better position in the job market.

Table 4.2 The number of Zhiqing returning to the city through various channels (1976–79)

Year	Zhiqing returned to the city	Different channels of return			
		Higher education	Conscription	Job recruitment	Other
1976	1,350,000	73,000	112,700	992,400	170,300
1977	1,030,000	79,000	55,700	694,400	197,800
1978	2,550,000	270,900	298,100	1,307,800	666,400
1979	3,950,000	89,100	90,400	2,788,100	1,471,100
Total	8,880,000	512,000	556,900	5,782,700	2,505,600

Source: From Liu 1998b; and Bonnin 2009; reproduced with permission from Chinese University Press

Due to the emergency of nationwide protests, the UMDC Movement was halted abruptly. At this point urban society was not ready to accommodate tens of millions of Zhiqing. This immediately caused enormous pressure on urban employment and the administration of household residence (户口).

In 1979, there were about 20 million urban residents waiting for job allocation, of whom 3.95 million were Zhiqing, including those who had just returned to the city and those who had returned before but were still unemployed. Apart from them, there were millions of Zhiqing in the countryside waiting to return to the city. In order to create more jobs, the state took certain economic measures, such as supporting light industry and service industry and encouraging collective and private businesses. Administrative measures like the "substitution policy" and "work unit responsibility" were also applied to increase employment.[3] The issue of unemployment had been alleviated by the end of 1982; however, most Zhiqing were allocated unstable and lower-income jobs in tiny collectively owned factories or private businesses, while only a few were employed by state-owned enterprises.

The other thorny issue of household residence was in fact intertwined with the issue of employment. According to the strict household registration system, a permanent urban residence matched strictly with a job in the city. In order to get their legal residence, Zhiqing had little choice but to accept whatever was available to them. For married Zhiqing, the situation was even worse because they had to deal with the extra trouble of getting permanent urban residence for their spouse and children.[4] As a consequence, family separation and other related problems became a major residual issue of the UMDC Movement.

From the above review, it can be deduced that: 1 the abrupt termination of the UMDC Movement was a compromise between the state and society, made under particular political, social and historical circumstances; 2 measures implemented in response to the emergent situation have proven insufficient for fundamental structural reasons (e.g. education, economy and the registered permanent residence system); 3 after their return, Zhiqing suffered from inferior social economic status, later-life inequalities and disadvantages, as well as discrimination and alienation in urban society. As a significant event, Zhiqing's massive retreat and hasty resettlement shaped their life course and had long-term effects on their later lives. This will be explained in detail in the following sections.

4.2 Limited education

Fundamentally, Zhiqing's disadvantageous position in urban society should be attributed to structural problems, especially the underdeveloped economy and the urban–rural gap. However, Zhiqing themselves often perceived this issue as a personal or generational drawback, namely a consequence of their limited education.

Most of the Zhiqing were assigned to simple labour work in small collectively owned factories and workshops, which affected their ability and motivation for continuing education. To them, their limited education and disadvantaged socio-economic status formed a vicious circle. The negative effects were most evident in the late 1990s and early 2000s when Zhiqing bore the brunt of the nationwide layoffs. At that time, those worker-peasant-soldier students who received higher education were in a relatively better situation. Nevertheless, their positions were challenged as well when the recommendation criterion and education quality were questioned after the resumption of the university entrance examination. After graduation, interviewee 29 found a lectureship at a college. She remembered the pressure of being marginalized as a worker-peasant-soldier student at the beginning of her career. Then, she decided to pursue a higher degree to improve her inferior status:

> The college was newly established, so many old university graduates[5] were transferred from other cities to Shanghai [to set up the faculty]. They were old intellectuals. In front of them, I felt inferior anyhow as a "barefoot" student ... I thought I couldn't let myself be eliminated, so I prepared to sit the examination for [the] undergraduate course.

As explained in Chapter 2, education is an important element of life chances. Its significance became evident when Zhiqing returned to the city and then gradually intensified due to the cumulative effect of socio-economic status. According to social identity theory, attributes that highlight intergroup differences would be exaggerated (Tajfel's Law) and characteristics of an outgroup are assumed to be negative (Turner's motivational explanation). Therefore, Zhiqing's disadvantage in education has not only socio-economic but also cognitive and cultural implications. In this sense, common ideas of Zhiqing being "poorly educated", "less-competitive" and "incapable" are not simply representations of socio-economic facts, but are also stereotyped notions generated by intergroup comparisons. More importantly, as Rupert Brown pointed out, when stereotypes are accepted as conventional ideas by most social members, their constructive function would come into play, particularly in terms of justifying intergroup prejudices and legitimizing established structural inequalities. Personal hatred and group conflicts in a society can often be traced to certain conventional ideas which are believed to be reasonable and righteous but are in fact created and manipulated by the intertwined influences of social-structural forces and constructive social cognition. Zhiqing's life experiences thus could be seen as convincing evidence of these arguments.

4.3 The difficult settling-in phase

As explained earlier, the settling-in phase after Zhiqing's Massive Retreat was hasty and difficult. First and foremost, Zhiqing had to find a job to make a living. Due to the special circumstance at that time, they had to accept whatever was assigned to them. Frustrations in the job market gave rise to a common feeling of dissatisfaction and helplessness, as interviewee 3 described:

> When I got back [to the city], well, I just felt that my job was not ideal because it was not my choice. While working in that factory, with the loud noise from those machines, I sometimes felt: gosh, you could die right away at this place. I just felt like that because this was not what I wanted. You couldn't change it. You had returned from the countryside, you should appreciate it. Besides, there was no other choice either.

Many interviewees believed that education was the key influence that determined their position in urban society. Others also mentioned family background as a major factor. Interviewee 1 graduated from a key university during the UMDC Movement, yet she could not get the job she wanted because her family was not "well connected".

> If you have connections you could be able to find a way out, but I hadn't many options, so I simply accepted my fate ... Zhiqing were unemployed youth when they first returned, they had to find jobs through all kinds of relationships. If a Zhiqing had a powerful family, his/her situation would be better. Mine was not too bad, but [the process] was still quite tortuous. It took great troubles.

Education and human capital (mainly family background) are determinant factors of life chances. To the entire Zhiqing group, the low level of education largely restricted all members' access to pursuing better opportunities. On the individual level, the actual impact varied to a certain extent due to Zhiqing's different family backgrounds.

As interviewee 1 pointed out, a few individuals benefited from their family connections in the settling-in phase in terms of employment, permanent urban residence and other welfare. Nevertheless, these temporary benefits do not necessarily guarantee advantageous positions in later life stages or overall higher socio-economic status. For example, those who entered state-owned enterprises "through the back door" were generally laid off in their late thirties or forties and encountered retrogression of socio-economic status. This shows that life chances and the related status should be understood

Drops of water in the ocean 65

from a longitudinal and comprehensive perspective by taking into consideration changes over time and all possible factors.

As the life course analysis in Chapter 2 shows, most Zhiqing suffered from the delayed and low starting point of socio-economic accumulation as well as structural restrictions to self-development later. As perceived by the rest of society, Zhiqing's disadvantaged status is normally regarded as the tragedy of the entire group, rather than individuals' misfortune. This suggests that in terms of life chances and socio-economic status, structural forces, such as social categorization and societal changes, are more fundamental than human resources and other (inter)personal factors.

In their entire life course, Zhiqing underwent two settling-in phases at different historical times. They encountered different challenges in the two phases, which accordingly influenced the group-identity configuration in different ways. While resettling in urban society, Zhiqing engaged with the other contrasting group in the grey zone, i.e. urban citizens. As a consequence, the ingroup-outgroup boundary was redrawn and certain latent group prototypes were activated during this process, causing changes to the group-identity configuration. Similar to what had happened in the former settling-in phase, those deep transformations were manifested mainly in the following two life transitions.

4.3.1 From farm work to careers in the city

Like the farm work in the countryside, workplaces in the city constituted an important field where intergroup interactions took place. Through the daily work, the ingroup-outgroup meta-contrast became perceivable and relevant to individuals, and thereby stimulated their identification processes and behaviours. There are also critical differences between the two settling-in phases. The Zhiqing-peasants meta-contrast of the first phase was more like a formal differentiation, compared with the meta-contrast between Zhiqing and urban citizens which had evaluative and discriminative connotations. As discussed, these connotations were closely associated with group-based stereotypes which had profound structural and cognitive origins.

4.3.2 From a Zhiqing-peasant relationship to a Zhiqing-urban citizen relationship

In urban society, Zhiqing's encounters with urban citizens (the outgroup) activated prototypes drawn from the peasants group. These include particular living habits, ways of thinking, behavioural patterns and personalities which they had acquired during the time in the countryside. For example, a lot of interviewees associated their career achievements with their UMDC experiences. Interviewee 19 worked extremely hard in Inner Mongolia and was promoted as a cadre. She believed that her career success in Shanghai benefited from the management experience that she had acquired in Inner Mongolia.

> Throughout my career life, I kept benefiting from what I had learnt in the countryside... In less than half a year, I got promoted to the Party Committee Office in the factory to take charge of organization works. It [what I had learnt in the countryside] played a key role in that period. In the Party Committee Office, you normally dealt with factory directors. They wouldn't buy it if you were not good enough. I did it well, using the experience I gained in the countryside... There was a phenomenal redundancy in 2006. Large numbers of workers were laid off for lacking certificates or because of their age. I stayed in my position until retirement, just because of my capability. I am very proud of that. [I made it] simply by relying on my experience in the countryside.

A frequently mentioned common factor was the hard-working spirit. Again, interviewees attributed it to their UMDC experiences. For example, after recalling how she took pains to prepare examinations for a higher degree, interviewee 29 summarized that "my experience in the countryside influenced my later life profoundly". Then she mentioned two other personality traits, a grateful heart and a strong sense of satisfaction, both of which had been developed in the countryside and then influenced her career in the city:

> I always feel that I should be grateful to what I already had because of my experience in the countryside. I feel indebted to my institute because I got a larger apartment than other lecturers. [So] I just work very hard. I once thought about transferring to Shanghai campus to mind my children, but I felt embarrassed [to make that request] because I had benefited a lot from my institute... Whenever I run into problems, I always think from another perspective and I always have a strong sense of satisfaction. At the early stage of my career, I was discriminated [against] because of my identity as a worker-peasant-soldier student. Sometimes I regret not attending a postgraduate school. Why didn't I have such an ambition? I felt regretful but maybe I was just satisfied [with the status quo] because I used to live in the countryside.

The above quotations illustrate that while being reviewed by interviewees, group prototypes were assigned with positive values. According to social identity theory, this is driven by the motivation for positive distinctiveness, which is particularly strong for people of inferior position in social comparison.

Drops of water in the ocean 67

To summarize: the two settling-in phases had the same form but different socio-political implications. As outsiders, Zhiqing sought to fit in the receiving society by engaging with the latter in both cases. In the former settling-in phase, Zhiqing felt strange and confused, while in the latter phase they struggled with the sense of inferiority and alienation. The comparison of the two settling-in phases demonstrates that the micro-level group-identity configuration is embedded in the macro social-historical process in which the structural and cognitive dimensions of that configuration process are interrelating and interacting in a dialectical way.

4.4 Blend into urban society

If resettlement was about finding a foothold in urban society, blending in involved efforts of socio-economic status enhancement and cultural integration. Interviewees' life stories demonstrate that Zhiqing experienced economic marginalization and cultural discrimination during that difficult process.

4.4.1 Discrimination against Zhiqing

Interviewee 25 gave an example of ordinary urban citizens' hostile attitudes towards Zhiqing.

> I came back to Shanghai in January of 1975. At that time, it was extremely unfair and unjust for Zhiqing . . . One day a female colleague said: "Things used to be fine in Shanghai; then everywhere became crowded since you guys came back." I was still young then, less than 40. I went mad after hearing that. I said: "You shouldn't say that. Let me tell you: if we hadn't gone to the countryside, you wouldn't be enjoying your life today." They were all shocked. So was she. She didn't expect that her careless words would enrage me. In fact, I had no problem with her personally. This was actually a reflection of unfair judgements we received from the whole society. They had this prejudice that Zhiqing brought many troubles to the city.

Then interviewee 25 further explained economic and cultural foundations for the prejudice against Zhiqing:

> Large numbers of Zhiqing returned to the city in 1979. Most of them ended up in collectively owned work places. This categorization of Zhiqing based on the ownership of our work places was a reflection of the unfairness we suffered from in the urban society. Later, that

categorical label caused troubles in spouse selection. Luckily I am a woman. Men would have big trouble if they were not employed by a state-owned work place, because other jobs were regarded as less stable and as having lower welfare. That was it . . . Therefore, I was really upset then. I wondered why we were treated like third-class citizens.

To understand fully the discrimination against Zhiqing, it is vital to identify its nature and origin. First, this was an intergroup discrimination, even though it could be experienced as personal conflict in everyday interactions. Based on minimal group experiments, Tajfel argues that intergroup discriminations could be triggered as long as the categorical differentiation is perceived by individual members. In other words, the foundation of intergroup discrimination lies in the salience of categorical memberships, not in personal values preferences. This explains interviewees' different opinions about the discrimination against Zhiqing. Interviewee 25 represented those who believed that they suffered from disadvantages, unfairness and discrimination simply because Zhiqing were perceived as different from other urban residents. Some other interviewees disagreed with this idea. For instance, interviewee 21 argued that: "I didn't feel any discrimination. Anyhow, there was nothing special about Zhiqing. The whole generation was like that." By "nothing special", he meant that Zhiqing had no particular attributes that would cause discrimination. Obviously, he understood the concept of discrimination in terms of interpersonal relations and missed the critical matter that Zhiqing were discriminated against not because of who they were but simply because of who they were not – that is, the urban citizen membership they lost during the UMDC Movement, which later marked them as others to the urban society.

Second, this intergroup discrimination originated from social categorization which itself was generated by structural forces. According to social identity theory, social categorization triggers the depersonalization process, at the end of which the depersonalized individuals would no longer be treated by their personal attributes but rather by their memberships.[6] As illustrated by interviewee 25's words, the discrimination she faced was not personal ("had no problem with her personally"), but was "a reflection of the unfairness we suffered from in the urban society". More importantly, the depersonalization is a cognitive process through which group norms and prototypes are internalized as part of the individual's self-concept. Consequently, driven by the depersonalized self-concept, individuals would think and behave in accordance with their group norms and prototypes, and discriminate against outgroup members for they are the others. In this sense, cultural discrimination is more subtle and profound than economic marginalization because

Drops of water in the ocean 69

it is stereotypes internalized as part of individuals' cognition, and more importantly because it was constructive perception that justifies intergroup prejudice and legitimizes established structural inequalities.

4.4.2 Coping with discrimination

The above review and analysis focus on social evaluation of Zhiqing and underlying discourses and power relations. To understand the group-identity configuration comprehensively, it is equally important to investigate Zhiqing's attitudes towards social evaluation and their own perceptions of the group, its prototypes and membership. Since the social evaluation was overwhelmingly negative, the question is mainly about how Zhiqing coped with the inferior social status and discrimination. As illustrated by quotations above, interviewees claimed that certain positive characteristics they gained in the countryside had significant influence on their later lives in the city. In most of the collected life stories, these influential positive characteristics were deemed as Zhiqing's unique features and were often highlighted by narrators in the context of Zhiqing-urban citizen comparisons.

One of the often-mentioned specialities is diligence and endurance, which were ascribed to the extremely difficult life in the countryside. Another example is the abundant life experience. In this context, days in the countryside were interpreted as Zhiqing's "indispensible wealth", as interviewee 15 said:

> This was indispensible wealth in our lives. You cannot buy it with money. Through it, you learnt how to deal with other things and how to handle problems in proper ways. It was worthwhile as it enriched your life experience. It is the wealth that today's young people are lacking. This is the reason why their thoughts are different from ours, right?

In this kind of narration, causal reasoning and comparison were often used together to demonstrate the uniqueness of Zhiqing's merits. On one hand, narrators would declare the causality between experiences in the countryside and certain positive characteristics; on the other hand, they would state urban citizens' lack of these traits. For example, interviewee 18 argued that compared with her classmates who stayed in Shanghai, Zhiqing had a broader vision and an open mind because they had seen more during the UMDC Movement.

> My classmates have never been out of Shanghai. Their personalities and behaviours are different from mine accordingly. What are their

shortcomings? They are relatively selfish since they wouldn't think about people in the countryside. We would care about people in the countryside but they wouldn't. They consider more for their own families and themselves. This is the difference because we've seen that there are so many people living such a hard life but they didn't.

Others like interviewee 28 thought that due to the UMDC experience, Zhiqing formed a personality that is different from and more pleasant than that of urban citizens.

> If it were not for the ten years in the countryside, and if I were in a factory in Shanghai, it would have been different... You know, peasants are practical and realistic. Those from factories, enterprises or public institutions in Shanghai are double-tongued. They are very sophisticated, yet we are simple minded. However, we are more generous and more considerate. We feel that we are forthright just like northerners. Those who haven't been to the countryside are totally different. The formation of our personalities is associated with this experience.

A more subtle difference lies in lifestyle, such as different consumption patterns, as illustrated by interviewee 27:

> My eldest sister stayed in Shanghai. Her consumption view is different from mine. She would like to eat out and take taxis all the time. I wouldn't take a taxi unless I have no choice, e.g. if I am carrying heavy bags. Perhaps because I have endured hardships in the countryside, I cherish today's life. I would never waste anything or pursue luxurious things. She had been dependent on our parents until she got married in her thirties. I've been completely relying on myself since I was 17.

The above quotations demonstrate that Zhiqing's self-perceptions are different from or even opposite to the social evaluation of the group. Obviously this does not mean that they did not realize their disadvantaged social position while suffering from economic marginalization and cultural discrimination. This is adopted as a strategy for coping with their inferiority in social comparisons. According to social identity theory, relative deprivation is a common coping strategy used by inferior groups. In practical terms, group members would restrict the scope or change the object of comparison so as to achieve preferable comparative results and minimize the sense of relative deprivation. This means that they would establish their own evaluative standard, rather than referring to socially acknowledged values. The above quotations reveal that interviewees relied on their own evaluative principle while emphasizing Zhiqing's "unique merits", which demonstrate their management of relative deprivation in offsetting their inferior social status.

There are also other strategies. As pointed out by social identity theorists, members of an inferior group may distance themselves from the group, i.e. lowering the degree of identification so as to be immune to negative comparative results. This explains why Zhiqing has been a silent and invisible group since the end of the UMDC Movement, just like interviewee 29's metaphor: "a drop of water in the sea." This situation started to change in the last ten years when Zhiqing-themed collective activities became popular around the country. Focusing on this specific phenomenon, the next section will discuss its origin and implications for the group-identity configuration.

4.5 Zhiqing-themed collective activities

Chapter 3 analysed Zhiqing's collective life in the countryside and revealed that the contextual shift from the individual mode to the collective mode activated the group-identity configuration which eventually led to individuals' identification with the Zhiqing group. At the time when Zhiqing were resettling in the city, the contextual shift took place again but in the opposite direction: from the collective/group mode to the individual mode. At that time, Zhiqing hardly had any collective activities. As interviewee 3 explained, "[d]uring these ten years after we just got married, we didn't meet very often because we were busy with our families, children and careers".

The so-called "Zhiqing cultural upsurge" (知青文化热) in the 1990s made the Zhiqing group and the Zhiqing identity prominent to the whole society. Then in the last decade, Zhiqing's collective activities began to flourish again. From the life course perspective, timing is a major factor for the prosperity of Zhiqing's collective activities. First of all, many Zhiqing retired in the 1990s and most of them have entered old age in the last ten years. Hence they have time and the financial capacity to organize and participate in collective activities. Second, the national economy has developed greatly since the implementation of the Reform and Open policy, which provided Zhiqing with better resources and economic environment for their collective activities.

In addition to these objective factors, collective activities are also propelled by social psychological reasons, which according to social identity theory are in fact legacies of the Zhiqing group, including group solidarity and individuals' commitment and behavioural conformity. In interviewees' life stories, group solidarity is often shown as the emotional ties they built up during the UMDC Movement. For example, many interviewees considered that their frequent get-togethers were based on genuine friendship they had established in the countryside, as interviewee 3 described: "Well, there is no taboo between us. No matter you are a senior officer or a successful businessman, when we are together, we forget all about that. It's still the original pure feelings we had at that time." A more powerful expression is the "Zhiqing complex" which interviewees usually used to justify the emotional basis of their collective activities. Interviewee 27 described her interpretation of the Zhiqing complex and explained how it had influenced their collective activities:

> Let me tell you something about the Zhiqing complex. The cohesive force of Zhiqing group derives from this complex. I think now we get together just because of this complex. Many people are there just because of that affection. Consequently, Zhiqing have a strong cohesive force ... The more often we gather, the closer our connections are.

A lot of Zhiqing invest much time and energy in collective activities and they believe that they received practical benefits and/or they made contributions to the community. Based on her experience and observation, interviewee 27 summarized the benefits of joining Zhiqing-themed collective activities.

> Generally speaking, Zhiqing is a disadvantaged group. A large number of Zhiqing now live difficult lives. We encourage each other in these activities ... You see, we are over 60 now but we are still dancing and we are very busy every day. In our post-Zhiqing lives, we are seeking happiness for ourselves and by ourselves because there aren't many joyful things in other area ... To be honest, people like me have nothing to do other than participating in these activities. What would you do today? I would simply do some grocery shopping, laundry work and cooking, right? You would be bored with that kind of life. Through these activities, you could enrich your life and activate your mentality. With an up-coming activity, you then have something to hope for.

Obviously, these practical benefits, such as mutual aid in problem solving and the sense of fulfilment and happiness, are based on individuals' interdependence which is the essence of emotional ties. Solidarity and emotional connection, according to Horwitz and Rabbie, manifest the cohesiveness of the Zhiqing group, a legacy that keeps influencing individual members' lives in the post-movement era.

Other interviewees perceive Zhiqing-themed collective activities differently. Their experiences and ideas demonstrate individuals' commitment to each other and to the entire group. Interviewee 25 was a member of a Zhiqing association in Shanghai. From her position as an organizer, she explained how collective activities could be used to provide enlightenment and spiritual support to Zhiqing.

> We focus on organizing tours – cultural tours . . . we consciously learn things and review them in our tours. It is not just about having fun but also out of a sense of responsibility, namely bringing [this sort of education] to Zhiqing and to influence them . . . A large number of Zhiqing are now living with a minimum income and they end up in playing Mahjong, drinking and complaining. My hope is to pull them out of that condition. I think a main theme in the post-Zhiqing era is to do things useful to the society, to our group and to individual . . . I think the whole society should pay attention to and help Zhiqing based on sympathy. I am doing my bit as well. You've got to have some spiritual pursuit.

Another active participant, interviewee 26, believed that through collective activities, Zhiqing could further develop academic research and cultural creation, and thereby contribute to the whole nation:

> We put forward a slogan: "Prosper Zhiqing Culture" [繁荣知青文化]. We think that Zhiqing's contributions are far from exhaustion . . . I think it is meaningful to organize retired Zhiqing to do historical and cultural research and literary and artistic creation. It's a record of our experiences and ideas. It is a cultural heritage for our offspring

As shown in the quotations, by participating in and contributing to collective activities, Zhiqing fulfil their responsibility and commitment to each other, to the entire group and also to the whole society.

Viewing the two stages of the group-identity configuration together, it is clear that group solidarity and individuals' commitment have played equally significant roles in the activation and functioning of the configuration process as well as in the maintenance/continuity of its effects/legacies. As emphasized in Chapter 3, in order to understand their different foundations and effects, it is vital to analyse phenomena of solidarity and commitment in specific contexts. So far, the analysis has focused on prosperity and positive implications of Zhiqing-themed collective activity. A comprehensive understanding must also consider the complexity and especially the limitations of these activities in the current social context.

First of all, the Zhiqing group has become fragmented and stratified, just as interviewee 17 pointed out: "Of course we don't differentiate each other while we are sitting together in these activities. However, it is completely different in real life. At our gatherings, we just have this tacit understanding – we would not mention this." This "tacit understanding" coexists with interviewee 3's perception of the "original pure feelings", suggesting the complex nature of the Zhiqing group in the post-movement era. The complexity also reveals an essential deficit of those Zhiqing-themed collective activities. Despite their psychological and cultural significance, they rarely challenge the established social and institutional arrangements which are largely accountable for Zhiqing's disadvantaged status.

Second, Zhiqing also developed a more rational and selective attitude as they became more familiar with these collective activities. Smaller groups have formed within large inclusive networks. According to interviewee 28, this "cluster effect" is a natural outcome of frequent collective activities:

> If we could get along with each other, we would keep on that relationship. In the last two years, we haven't had big events but only small-scale activities ... People do cluster. That's for sure. Because those [with] similar characters and thoughts would contact each other more often ... At first, we were relatively more excited. Now you would pick those more interesting activities or choose to meet some people you haven't seen for a long time.

Lastly and most importantly, the Zhiqing group has dissolved since the end of the UMDC Movement. Thus collective activities are no longer the centre of individual Zhiqing's life as they used to be. Similarly, the group solidarity and members' commitment as well as other legacies of the group-identity configuration would become salient only in particular circumstances, such as Zhiqing-themed collective activities.

4.6 Zhiqing's personal relationships

Zhiqing's personal relationships in urban society mainly include connections with other Zhiqing, in marital and parent-children relationships. Most Zhiqing have maintained close relationships with each other and regard their relationships as of siblings. This proves the continuity of the group cohesiveness and individuals' identification.[7]

4.6.1 Marital relationship

According to the data in Liu (1998b, 867), the majority of Zhiqing were still single when they returned to the city. At that time, they had already passed the best age of spouse selection. Delayed marriage is a typical example of structural lag caused by the UMDC Movement. From a structural and historical view, marriage issues often reflect societal problems and social transformation. In terms of Zhiqing's marriage, socio-historical influences are manifested by specific problems of the three marriage types: Zhiqing-peasant marriage, Zhiqing-urban worker marriage, and Zhiqing-Zhiqing marriage.

Zhiqing-peasant marriage

According to Liu (1998b), the majority of the Zhiqing who got married in the countryside wed local peasants.[8] Interviewees' narrations suggest that this kind of marriage was marginalized or even despised. Interviewee 3 stated that these individuals were regarded as inferior by the rest of the Zhiqing group.

> Few individuals could not bear the hardship, so they went to villagers' homes. After all, they were families, so their situations were relatively better. We felt that they were weak-willed persons. They found local peasants and simply married them. Only a few individuals couldn't bear the hardships.

Her perception also indicates that some Zhiqing chose to marry peasants for practical concerns: to make a living under the difficult circumstances. From 1972, every year there were a certain amount of Zhiqing who returned to the city in different ways. Being desperate to go home, some married Zhiqing simply abandoned their families in the countryside. When the Massive Retreat happened in the late 1970s, those who married peasants had problems in getting permanent urban residence for their countryside spouses and children. This caused a large number of divorces and other forms of family separation.

Interviewee 3's opinion represents a general prejudice of Zhiqing-peasant marriages. As a matter of fact, negative stereotypes of the Zhiqing-peasant marriage were an embodiment of the Zhiqing-peasant differentiation and the urban-rural dual system. Group members who married outsiders (peasants) were treated as "black sheep" by the entire group because of the actual and symbolic violation their marriage caused to the Zhiqing-peasant (ingroup-outgroup) meta-contrast.

Zhiqing-urban worker marriage

In the 1980s, marrying a worker meant marrying someone of stable income and creditable social status. For Zhiqing, this was an upward marriage. In his research paper on Zhiqing marriage, Zhao (2009) argues that the low percentage of Zhiqing-worker marriages among the three marriage types demonstrates significant influence of the urban-rural dual structure on spouse selection. He also points out that it was easier for female Zhiqing to marry "up" to urban worker husbands than the other way round. This was mentioned by interviewee 25 as well. As she recalled, male Zhiqing "would have big trouble if they were not employed by a state-owned work place". In the urban "marriage market", Zhiqing were less competitive than urban citizens of their age group. Obviously, this civil and cultural disadvantage was a result of Zhiqing's marginalized socio-economic position in urban society. Under these circumstances, many Zhiqing had to lower their standards and expectations of spouse selection. Interviewee 3 described how she made her choice with an evident mood of regret.

> When I came back to work, I was about 23 or 24, so I was trying to find my mate in a hurry. I got married at 25. I married a soldier. It was good enough at that time to marry a soldier and Party member. Now I am regretful about it. I felt that I was a worker, so I lowered my expectation. I was a worker, and he was a soldier and Party member. So I didn't look for anyone else. That was it. In fact we are not so suitable for each other in terms of our characters and other aspects.

Later in their lives, problems of Zhiqing-worker marriages gradually emerged. While talking about their marriages, many interviewees emphasized differences with their spouses. Very often, they attributed their divergences and family disputes to their different life experiences, especially their spouses' lack of UMDC experience. For instance, interviewee 15 underlined disagreements he had with his wife on several social issues such as the inflow of migrant workers to the city:

> I give more sympathy to peasants while she would always criticize those migrant workers. I said that everyone would like to live a better life. They had no choice. So I feel naturally sympathetic to peasants. However, as an urban resident, she seems to have an instinctive feeling of hostility towards them. She complains a lot about them rushing into the city and competing with urban residents for jobs and so on. I keep telling her that it is not right to think so.

Interviewee 28 complained that she shared little in common with her husband, in terms of their viewpoints, personalities and behaviours, simply because he was not a Zhiqing.

> He didn't go to the countryside. We have completely different viewpoints. It is a pity for me. I should have found a guy who had been to the countryside. We are very innocent and honest, he is quite shrewd . . . I [get] involve[ed] in the society actively. He doesn't like participating

in social activities. Zhiqing are different. We have gatherings and other activities, which is in fact beneficial to yourself.

Sometimes, Zhiqing-themed activities would become an issue in family disputes. Interviewee 19 said she was happy enough that her husband "understands that we lived a hard life there and that local villagers took care of us and hence we had this emotional tie". However, her husband still "doesn't like that we get together all the time, and he wouldn't participate in these activities". Interviewee 27 expressed directly her discontent with her husband: "I envy those Zhiqing couples. If one goes to Zhiqing reunion or activities, the other wouldn't disagree. He gets so annoyed when we have frequent activities. He often complains that we keep talking about Zhiqing all the time."

The above quotations[9] demonstrate that marital relationships could be examined as a field of intergroup engagement. In this context, interviewees tended to attribute family disputes to their different group memberships as well as the fundamental categorical differentiation between the Zhiqing group and other social groups.

Zhiqing-Zhiqing marriage

A few Zhiqing had stable relationships in the countryside and got married there or soon after they returned to the city. However, affections were not the only foundation for Zhiqing-Zhiqing marriages. Many interviewees claimed that their marriages with other Zhiqing were out of practical concerns. In interviewee 17's description, it seems that his marriage was out of frustration after return rather than their emotional ties:

> We were quite ignorant when we went [to the countryside]. We were only 16 then and we didn't know anything. During those years in the production team, we didn't communicate very often. It was only after 1976 when we had to face the truth, because those who were able to leave had gone . . . I came back to Shanghai in 1978, she came back in 1979 and we got married in 1980.

Interviewee 21 married a Zhiqing of the same corps. He argued that Zhiqing couples' same experiences did not necessarily result in joyful relationships or happy marriages because "[y]ou don't have many options in the countryside, right? There were just these people in the corps. A lot of people got together because there weren't other choices".

Contrarily, other interviewees also pointed out that many Zhiqing did deliberately look for people of similar UMDC experiences. For example, interviewee 1 said: "many people tended to look for Zhiqing as their spouses in consideration of their same experience and the common language." Compared with the above two types of marriage, intergroup conflict would not be an issue in Zhiqing-Zhiqing marriages. Interviewee 17 gave an example of the support he received from his wife who was also a Zhiqing.

> My wife never says anything whenever I go out to attend Zhiqing activities. You see, we set up a foundation. We raised 250,000 yuan RMB to help poor students. I contributed 10 per cent of that money. The money is used to help disadvantaged Zhiqing in Shanghai and poor children in Ai'hui [Heilongjiang province]. She never complained a single word. If she were not Zhiqing, she would have gone like: "Taken money out from your family, are you kidding?" Right? She never complains. This is our Zhiqing complex. We have experienced that together.

Interviewee 17's personal experience should not be generalized as a common situation of the entire Zhiqing group. In a cognitive and psychological sense, however, the perception of harmonious Zhiqing-Zhiqing marriages could be seen as a reflection of individual Zhiqing's ingroup favouritism. According to Tajfel, ingroup favouritism is not based on individuals' personal attributes or preferences, but is contingent upon social comparison and intergroup differentiation. This explains why ingroup favouritism is also influential in private spheres like Zhiqing's marital relationships.

Apart from this social-psychological perspective, interviewees' contradictory opinions about Zhiqing-Zhiqing marriage should also be understood in the social-historical context. Whether it was an active choice or out of frustration, marrying another Zhiqing was an acceptable and realistic option. From the historical view, it is clear that regardless of the specific marriage type, Zhiqing's marital relationships were generally based more on pragmatic considerations, and less on emotional needs. Reasons were complicated. On one hand, the ignorance of these young people when they were living together in the countryside could be related to cultural factors, such as the suppression of human nature and especially the taboo of individualist desire for love, romance and sex in that particular historical period. On the other hand, frustrations and conflicts of Zhiqing's marital relationships were largely due to social-structural problems, such as structural lag of personal development and intergroup discrimination.

4.6.2 Parent-child relationships

Compared with the older generations, Zhiqing experienced an evident structural lag in terms of the delay of their marriage, childbearing and other transitional life events. Besides, the UMDC experiences also left impacts on Zhiqing's parent-child relationships, the significance of which is vividly illustrated by the following three frequently mentioned issues in interviewees' life stories.

Fulfilling parents' dreams

While reviewing their later lives in the city, many interviewees expressed a strong sense of relative deprivation. A high-frequency term, "the lost generation", in their narrations suggests that besides looking for social-structural reasons, interviewees also tended to perceive their disadvantaged status as a generational issue. For instance, many interviewees emphasized the coincidence between their life transition and significant socio-historical events, which they believed had resulted in their current situation as an unfortunate generation. It is thus understandable that many Zhiqing would transfer their hopes and desires to their children. Interviewee 3 recalled how she devoted her love and energy to her daughter.

> I just wished that she could have things that I hadn't got. I put all my hope on her . . . I took her to learn musical instruments, dancing and foreign languages. I simply forced her to learn. I was very strict to her when she was small. I just hoped that she could reach further in education . . . I cherished her very much. She was the only child. I scrounged every penny to get her what she needed.

Another mother, interviewee 25, had a similar experience and she argued that this was in fact a common Zhiqing characteristic:

> I devoted almost all my hope while minding my child. I wished that she could fulfil everything that I failed to accomplish, like going to a university. That's absolutely without a doubt, and it must be one of the top universities. I kept encouraging her along the way like: "This is about achieving our mum's dream, right?" Anyway, for our generation, we simply wish our next generation could realize things we couldn't do when we were young.

Not every Zhiqing would acknowledge this "common characteristic", but from the life course perspective, it is vital to know the simple fact that impacts of the UMDC Movement are not limited to the Zhiqing generation but are also passed on to the next generation. This echoes a main argument of the life course theory that individuals' development paths are interrelated.

Passing on parents' experience

As is illustrated in former sections, Zhiqing perceive the UMDC Movement as the positive distinction that protects their self-esteem from being affected by their socio-cultural disadvantages.

In terms of parent-children relationships in particular, Zhiqing also show an enthusiasm in passing on their precious UMDC experience to their children, in the belief that it could benefit them as well. Interviewee 1 remembered having difficulties in the countryside for lacking certain life skills. Thus she insisted that her daughter should acquire those skills to avoid detours she once had.

> Before going to the countryside, we lived with our grandma, and my sister and I were brought up by a nanny. We didn't know how to do housework. While living in the countryside, others from multi-children families were capable of doing everything, so I felt I was disadvantaged in that aspect of my life. This notion has been very influential for me. Therefore, when my daughter was small, I tried my best to make her as independent as possible. It proved effective. My daughter is very independent.

While dealing with the structural lag and other residual problems of the UMDC Movement, interviewee 13 developed the notion that individuals should be independent and stand up to difficulties. He thought he had benefited from the experience and thus should pass it on to his son:

> During his internship, I told him that many things you owned could be taken away but there was one thing that no one could take away from you and that was your knowledge and your skills, right? I said you had to rely on yourself if you wanted to keep your foothold in this society. So my son truly believes in this. I told him that social distribution was never a once for all thing. Because this was your dad's own experience. Never presume that you could enjoy a well-off life just because you had a certificate from a good university. That's not how it works in this society . . . Now he is doing very well. His college is not so renowned. All he has today is gained by his efforts, so I think he is really brilliant. I believe that my education is successful.

According to Turner's motivational explanation, under the normative efficacy of a salient group membership, individuals will show evident ingroup favouritism by interpreting and practising formal intergroup differentiation in evaluative terms. In other words, categorical distinctions are assumed to be or even interpreted as positive or superior features. The above quotations show that experience individuals gained during the UMDC Movement was believed to be beneficial. Even difficulties and frustrations were regarded as worthwhile lessons for their children. Passing experience to the next generation is universal to all human beings. With regard to Zhiqing's parent-children relationships, the specificity lies in the historical and social-psychological contexts.

Intensified generation gap

Many interviewees complained about the difficulty of communicating their ideas and values with their children because of the generation gap. For instance, interviewee 19 talked about his feelings with a critical view on the younger generation:

> I rarely teach my child. There is a generational gap. He wouldn't understand what I told him. Why? He didn't have that experience. Historical conditions today are not comparable to those in the past. So his thoughts are completely different from mine. Nowadays most children emphasize objective restrictions but neglect their own initiatives. The society is developing towards this same trend as well.

Again, a generation gap is not unique to Zhiqing and their children. However, its actual significance and Zhiqing's perceptions could be more intense than they would be in other intergenerational relationships. A main reason for this intensified generation gap could be that the intergroup difference between Zhiqing and their children adds on to the influence of their generational differences. Besides, as pointed out by many interviewees, the generational differences have also been reinforced by profound social transformations in China in the Reform and Open era.

To summarize: parent-children relationships are an epitome of Zhiqing's complex nature as a particular generation and a special social group. Consequently, features and implications of Zhiqing's parent-children relationships ought to be understood from the integrated human developmental and social-structural perspectives.

4.7 Revisiting "second homes" in the countryside

Since their return, a few Zhiqing have maintained connections with the countryside. Some of them paid return visits to the villages in the 1980s. In the last ten years, return visits have become a main Zhiqing collective activity. Motivations for these return visits are complicated. In the 1980s and

1990s, it was mainly out of a nostalgic sentiment, as interviewee 2 said: "I had a sort of nostalgia about that period of time. However, it has passed after all. You couldn't be like that all the time. You simply couldn't stand it."

A more significant and enduring impetus is the emotional tie between Zhiqing and local villagers established during the UMDC Movement, which continues to bind them together in psychological and cultural senses. This emotional foundation is best illustrated by a metaphorical term, "the second home", which was frequently mentioned in most of the collected life stories. Interviewee 3 talked about her own experience and feelings about her second hometown: "We felt that we just wanted to visit our second home . . . I sang the song 'Fellow Villagers' just to express our feelings and emotions about the place and the people." In her visits, interviewee 16 felt the same way, but she believed that the emotional tie was universal to all Zhiqing, not just those who are keen on paying return visits.

> Not just me, even those who hate the UMDC Movement still have feelings about these villages they once lived in. There is one thing I think we share in common: connections and affections with the countryside. I think the main reason is that Zhiqing made selfless devotions there. Another reason is UMDC was a dividing line for us. We were students then, and we knew nothing about the society. Zhiqing's worldviews and values all took shape in that period. It left such deep imprints on our lives. These worldviews and values are still influencing our ways of thinking and other aspects of our lives.

Return visits are not just about sightseeing or reminiscence. By maintaining connections with the villages, some Zhiqing provide support or directly participate in economic and cultural development in the countryside. Interviewee 29 illustrated how Zhiqing helped local villagers to improve conditions:

> The outside world had been changing greatly, yet they were still so poor. I felt so sad about it during my first visit . . . When I left, I told them that they must build the road. I said: "I will never come back again if you don't build the road" . . . In that year, some young peasants from the village came to Shanghai to look for jobs. We helped them. A Zhiqing couple provided an apartment for them to live [in], and another couple who lived nearby usually visited them [and] cooked for them.

Chapter 3 analysed Zhiqing's short vacations at home, and concluded that those return visits shook the foundation of the Zhiqing group, the group cohesiveness and members' identification. By contrast, return visits to "the second home" reinforced Zhiqing's connection with the rural society and re-intensified the group membership that had been concealed in the post-UMDC era. The above quotations demonstrate two main motivations for Zhiqing's connection with their second homes: their emotional ties with local villagers and their commitment to the local rural society. As discussed in former chapters, emotional ties and commitment are the two origins of group cohesiveness. Therefore, from the perspective of social identity theory, the underlying causes of those return visits are not simply nostalgic sentiments but are the enduring effect of the group-identity configuration.

4.8 Summary

Focusing on the latter half of interviewees' life stories in the post-UMDC era, this chapter discussed special features of Zhiqing's group-identity configuration formed under different socio-historical circumstances.

Based on the analysis of their limited education in Chapter 3, this chapter further probed into this issue by revealing its cumulative effects on Zhiqing's later lives and analysing the social-structural and psychological factors for prejudice against Zhiqing. The chapter then looked into distinctions between the two settling-in phases under different social-historical circumstances and pointed out that the former settling-in phase resulted in formal differentiation between Zhiqing and peasants, while the latter one caused evaluative and hierarchical distinction between Zhiqing and urban citizens. Based on this notion, the chapter elaborated the origins of social discrimination against Zhiqing and Zhiqing's coping strategies. These two sections of this chapter and those in Chapter 3 constitute a comprehensive and diachronic analysis of Zhiqing's group-identity configuration.

The last three sections of this chapter investigated enduring effects of the UMDC experience on various aspects of Zhiqing's lives in the post-UMDC era. Based on social identity theory, analysis of these effects shed light on the continuity of the Zhiqing group and its cohesiveness as well as the salience of the Zhiqing identity under different circumstances.

Notes

1 See details of the process and official documentation in Chapter 2 of this book.
2 According to Michel Bonnin, the number of Zhiqing admitted through the University/College Entrance Examination and those admitted through recommendation were roughly the same. See Bonnin (2009, 178).
3 Substitution policy (Dingti zhidu 顶替制度): once a worker retires, his or her child was allowed to take the job. Work unit responsibility (Danwei baogan 单位包干): work units are responsible for providing jobs for their employees' children. See a more detailed introduction of the substitution policy and work unit responsibility in Bonnin (2009, 172–173).

4 See more details about married Zhiqing and problems with their household registration transfer in Zhao (2009, 500–508).
5 "Old graduates" refers to those who received their degrees or finished most of their courses before the explosion of the Cultural Revolution.
6 See Figure 1.1 in Chapter 1 of this book.
7 See also Chapter 3.
8 In Liu (1998b), the extent of Zhiqing-peasant marriages was 74.9 per cent in Jilin (1980) and 75.5 per cent in the Baoding area of Hebei (1978).
9 Interviewees' narration could be influenced by the topic of the interview (Zhiqing), and hence they would "consciously" associate their life experiences with that topic. In consideration of this, the above discussion referred to statistical and historical analyses by Liu (1994a) and Zhao (2009).

5 The identity of Zhiqing
Approach and conclusion

Before drawing conclusions to questions raised in Chapter 1, this chapter will start by clarifying the perspective, premise and principles of this study.

5.1 Approach: a dialectical and longitudinal study of the identity of Zhiqing

Identity is an umbrella concept. It is defined distinctly from different disciplinary perspectives in various contexts. Thus the identity of Zhiqing also ought to be understood in context and in time. Based on this premise, the authors approached the research topic from an integrated perspective and constructed the framework of analysis with social identity theory and life course theory. In the discussion part, the following principles were applied:

1 A social identity is by nature the gestalt of the formation and functioning of the relevant social group. Therefore, the identity of Zhiqing should be perceived as the Zhiqing group-identity configuration process, rather than a static object.
2 The gestalt would come into being only when its normative efficacy is internalized by individual group members. Hence the group-identity configuration is an integration of social construction and personal acquisition.
3 The Zhiqing group-identity configuration has been embedded in the intertexture of Zhiqing's developmental processes and social history.

The first principle clarifies the conceptualization of identity in this study according to social identity theory. The second and third principles exemplify the integrated dialectical and longitudinal approach which was adopted in accordance with the dual nature of the configuration process and its diachronic changes over developmental and historical times.

86 *The identity of Zhiqing*

5.2 Conclusions: the making and loss of the Zhiqing identity

Three key research questions were raised at the beginning of this book. On the basis of analyses in former chapters, answers to those questions could be summarized as follows.

5.2.1 Who are Zhiqing?

The term "the lost generation" suggests Zhiqing's particular position in the social history resulting from the UMDC Movement and its long-term effects. Life course analysis in Chapter 2 explained that Zhiqing's particular position should be examined based on thorough understanding of their developmental process, their particular position in social history as well as in the intertexture of the two. It also illustrated that within the Zhiqing generation, the three cohorts are characterized by their common features and profound differences, which should be attributed to each cohort's demographic and developmental traits as well as the UMDC Movement and other socio-structural forces.

5.2.2 How did Zhiqing perceive their identities during the movement and how do they perceive them now?

A social-psychological perspective was adopted to explain what it means (or meant) to be a Zhiqing during (or after) the UMDC Movement in terms of the perceived socio-structural implications and individuals' self-concepts.

The two stages of the group-identity configuration were analysed respectively in Chapter 3 and Chapter 4. Together, the two chapters illustrated distinctions and continuity between the two stages. During the UMDC Movement, the Zhiqing group was rigidly bounded. As the allocated group membership, the Zhiqing identity was also acquired by individuals at the same time. Normative efficacy of the Zhiqing identity was accomplished through social construction and internalization, which was manifested by the formation of group norms and prototypes, and members' conformity to them. Termination of the movement caused the disintegration of Zhiqing group. Subsequent societal and cultural transformations accelerated the fragmentation of the former group members. In the post-movement era, individual Zhiqing had to rely on themselves while coping with their disadvantaged social position and various forms of discrimination. Hence the group membership and Zhiqing identity remained latent most of the time and would only be salient under specific circumstances such as Zhiqing-themed collective activities. Similarly, normative efficacy of the Zhiqing identity could be prominent or underlying, depending on the particular circumstances. To be more specific, the Zhiqing identity would be activated by intergroup engagement and other forms of social comparison.

5.2.3 How have Zhiqing been coping with the breakage in their identification processes?

To both the Zhiqing group-identity configuration and Zhiqing's life trajectories, termination of the UMDC Movement was evidently a watershed event. However, the answer to the third question lies precisely in the continuity between the two stages of identification.

Analyses in Chapter 3 and Chapter 4 demonstrated that the end of the UMDC Movement was a contextual shift rather than a "breakage". Implications of this contextual shift are best illustrated by profound impacts of the grey zone on individual Zhiqing's identification behaviours. Based on thorough understanding of the contextual shift and the grey zone, the third question could be resolved. In the post-movement era, the Zhiqing identity would become salient once individuals' awareness of this membership is activated by group circumstances (in contrast to individual circumstances). In social comparisons, certain group norms and prototypes would become prominent and be practised by individuals so as to guarantee favourable comparative outcome for positive distinctiveness of the group and for individuals' self-esteem.

5.3 Research outcomes and significance

For its focus on identity issues, this book is an important contribution to the knowledge of Zhiqing, which is achieved through the dialectical analysis of socio-structural and cognitive elements of the topic and the longitudinal study of its changes over time.

The phenomenal progress that China has achieved in the last three decades owes much to Zhiqing's great efforts and contributions. This indicates that inquiries into the significant implications of the UMDC Movement and its products, namely the Zhiqing group and the Zhiqing identity, will contribute to the further enhancement of Chinese Studies. Nevertheless, Zhiqing and the UMDC Movement is by far a less studied topic. Following this study, more efforts ought to be made to reduce this gap.

For identity studies, this research provides a special case in China. Besides, its framework of analysis, which is composed of the longitudinal (life course approach) and the social-psychological (social identity theory) perspectives, is applicable to other social groups that are historically originated, socially determined, and culturally and contextually constructed like the Zhiqing group.

5.4 Directions for future research

A main objective of this book is to provide a solid foundation for more in-depth discussions on the identity of Zhiqing. Due to the specificities and complexity of this topic, future research would require more theoretical exploration and more empirical studies.

First of all, the concept of identity could be interpreted from other theoretical perspectives. Social identity theory would be less adequate when social comparison is not the dominant factor or the focus of research. To give an example, Sheldon Stryker's identity theory (Stryker and Burke 2000) offers another option for the conceptualization of identity and identification. The critical difference between the two theories is that social identity theory sees identities as group memberships formed by social comparisons while identity theory defines identities as social roles constructed through personal interactions. The socially formed Zhiqing identity is also taken by individuals as their roles through obtaining, redefining and reconstructing it in their everyday interactions. Therefore, identity theory would facilitate future studies on individuals' interpretation, acquisition and reconstruction of the Zhiqing identity.

This study analyses interviewees' life stories by treating them as individuals' reflections and representations of their life experiences – in particular, their group behaviours and identifications. Viewed from the perspective of identity theory, a life story is not only a text but also a context and an action of storytelling. Thereby, Zhiqing's life stories could be interpreted differently, using the approach of narrative analysis which focuses on the structure rather than the content of each story. This analysis approach investigates how a story was told and why it was told in that way by analysing socio-linguistic and structural features of that story. Through combining identity theory and narrative analysis, future research could further elaborate individuals' acquisition and construction of the Zhiqing identity.

Another direction for future study is to develop the life course analysis of the Zhiqing generation. As illustrated in this book, Zhiqing's life transitions echoed most of the significant transformations of Chinese society, making the Zhiqing generation a perfect object of life course research. Academics in Europe and America have made many studies of similar generations in their countries. A good example is Glen H. Elder's (1999) monograph, *Children of the Great Depression*. Much more effort should be made to improve the study of Zhiqing's life course. This is not only significant for Zhiqing studies, but also important for better understanding of human development in general. This book laid the foundation for the discussion of more specific topics, such as cross-cohort and intergenerational comparison, and comparison between Zhiqing's children and those of urban residents. Empirical studies could utilize longitudinal and cross-sectional statistics for quantitative research, which would be an important supplement to the qualitative interpretation in this book.

References

Berge, Bruce L. and Howard Lune. 2008 [1989]. *Qualitative Research Methods for Social Sciences*. Boston: Allyn & Bacon.

Bernstein, Thomas P. 1977. *Up to the Mountains and Down to the Villages: The Transfer of Youth from Urban to Rural China*. New Haven, CT: Yale University Press.

Bleicher, Josef. 1980. *Contemporary Hermeneutics: Hermeneutics as Method, Philosophy and Critique*. London: Routledge.

Bleicher, Josef. 1982. *The Hermeneutic Imagination*. London: Routledge & Kegan Paul.

Bonnin, Michel. 2009. *Shiluo de yidai: zhongguo de shangshanxiaxiang yundong 1968–1980* 失落的一代:中国的上山下乡运动 1968–1980 [Lost Generation: Up to the Mountains Down to the Countryside Movement in China, 1968–1980]. Translated by Annie Au-Yeung. Hong Kong: Chinese University Press.

Broaded, C. Montgomery. 1983. "Higher Education Policy Changes and Stratification in China." *The China Quarterly 93*: 125–137.

Broaded, C. Montgomery. 1990. "The Lost and Found Generation: Cohort Succession in Chinese Higher Education." *The Australian Journal of Chinese Affairs 23*: 77–95.

Brown, Rupert J. 2000 [1988]. *Group Processes: Dynamics within and between Groups*. Oxford: Blackwell.

Brown, Rupert J. and Gordon F. Ross. 1982. "The Battle for Acceptance: An Investigation into the Dynamics of Intergroup Behaviour", in *Social Identity and Intergroup Relations*, edited by Henri Tajfel, 155–178. Cambridge: Cambridge University Press.

Cao Zuoya. 2003. *Out of the Crucible: Literary Works about the Rusticated Youth*. Lanham, MD: Lexington Books.

Chen, Kevin and Cheng Xiaonong. 1999. "Comment on Zhou & Hou: A Negative Life Event with Positive Consequences?" *American Sociological Review 64(1)*: 37–40.

Chen Pichao. 1972. "Overurbanization, Rustication of Urban-Educated Youths, and Politics of Rural Transformation: The Case of China." *Comparative Politics 4(3)*: 361–386.

Chen Xiaoya 陈小雅. 1995. "'Laosanjie wenhuare' toushi" 老三届文化热透视 [A Perspective of the "Laosanjie Cultural Upsurge"]. *Dongfang* 东方 2: 45–49.

Chen, Yixin. 1999. "Lost in Revolution and Reform: The Socioeconomic Pains of China's Red Guards Generation, 1966–1996." *Journal of Contemporary China* 8(*21*): 219–239.

Creswell, J.W. 1994. *Research Design: Qualitative and Quantitative Approaches.* London: Sage.

Creswell, J.W. 1998. *Qualitative Inquiry and Research Design: Choosing among Five Traditions.* Thousand Oaks, CA: Sage.

Crouch, Mira and Heather McKenzie. 2006. "The Logic of Small Samples in Interview Based Qualitative Research." *Social Science Information 45*(*4*): 483–499.

Cui Wunian 崔武年 and Yan Huai 阎淮. 1986. "Tantan 'Laosanjie'" 谈谈 "老三届" [Talk about "Laosanjie"]. *Qingnian yanjiu* 青年研究 *4*: 1–4.

Cutcliffe, J. and H. MacKenna. 2002. "When Do We Know What We Know? Considering the Truth of Research Findings and the Craft of Qualitative Research." *International Journal of Nursing Studies 39*(*6*): 616–618.

Davis, Deborah. 1992. "'Skidding': Downward Mobility among Children of the Maoist Middle Class." *Modern China 18*(*4*): 410–437.

Ding Xiaohe 丁晓禾. 1998a. *Laosanjie zhaoge sanbuqu* 老三届朝歌三部曲 [Morning Mood Trilogy of Laosanjie]. Beijing: Zhonggong dangshi chubanshe 中共党史出版社.

Ding Yizhuang 定宜庄. 1998b. *Zhongguo Zhiqing shi: Chulan (1953–1968)* 中国知青史:初澜 (1953–1968) [History of Zhiqing in China: The Initial Wave (1953–1968)]. Beijing: Zhongguo shehui kexue chubanshe 中国社会科学出版社.

Du Honglin 杜鸿林. 1993. *Fengchao dangluo, 1955–1979: zhongguo zhishi qingnian shangshanxiaxiang yundong shi* 风潮荡落 (1955–1979) 中国知识青年上山下乡运动史 [Rise and Fall, 1955–1979: History of Zhiqing Go Up to the Mountains down to the Countryside Movement in China]. Shenzhen: Haitian chubanshe 海天出版社.

Du Honglin 杜鸿林. 1991. "Zhishi qingnian shangshanxiaxiang yundong de pingjia ji qi lishi mingyun" 知识青年上山下乡运动的评价及其历史命运 [An Evaluation of the Zhishi qingnian UMDC Movement and its Historical Destiny]. *Lilun yu xiandaihua* 理论与现代化 *6*: 34–36.

Elder, Glen H. 1999 [1974]. *Children of the Great Depression: Social Change in Life Experience.* Boulder: Westview Press.

Elder, Glen H. 2003. "The Emergence of Life Course Studies and Theory" (lecture, Academia Sinica, Taipei, 6 March).

Elliot, Jane. 2005. *Using Narrative in Social Research.* London: Sage.

Fang Yi 方奕. 1995. "Zhiqing yanjiu de xianzhuang yu weilai" 知青研究的现状与未来 [The Status Quo and the Future of Zhiqing Studies] *Zhongguo qingnian yanjiu* 中国青年研究 *2*: 32–35.

Gadamer, Hans-Georg. 1975. *Truth and Method.* London: Sheed & Ward.

Gadamer, Hans-Georg. 1976. *Philosophical Hermeneutics.* Translated and edited by David Linge. Berkeley: University of California Press.

Giele, Janet Z. and Glen H. Elder, eds. 1998. *Methods of Life Course Research: Qualitative and Quantitative Approaches.* London: Sage.

Glaser, Barney G., and Anselm L. Strauss. 1967. *The Discovery of Grounded Theory: Strategies for Qualitative Research.* Chicago: Aldine.

Gold, Thomas B. 1980. "Report from China: Back to the City: The Return of Shanghai's Educated Youth." *The China Quarterly 84*: 355–370.
Gold, Thomas B. 1991. "Youth and the State." *The China Quarterly* (Special Issue: The Individual and State in China) *127*: 594–612.
Gu Hongzhang 顾洪章, ed. 1997a. *Zhongguo zhishi qingnian shangshanxiaxiang shimo* 中国知识青年上山下乡始末 [The Whole Story of Zhiqing UMDC in China]. Beijing: Zhongguo jiancha chubanshe 中国检察出版社.
Gu Hongzhang 顾洪章, ed. 1997b. *Zhongguo zhishi qingnian shangshanxiaxiang dashiji* 中国知识青年上山下乡大事记 [The Memorabilia of Zhiqing UMDC in China]. Beijing: Zhongguo jiancha chubanshe 中国检察出版社.
Guba, Egon G. and Yvonna S. Lincoln. 1994. "Competing Paradigms in Qualitative Research", in *Handbook of Qualitative Research*, edited by N.K. Denzin and Y.S. Lincoln, 105–117. Thousand Oaks, CA: Sage.
Guo Dong 郭栋, Jin Dalu 金大陆, Yang Changzheng 杨长征. 1996. "Chengshi kuwa: guanyu jing jin hu 'huicheng zivn' wenti de duihua" 城市苦娃:关于京津沪知青"回城子女"问题的对话 [Poor Kids in the City: A Conversation on the Issue of "Returning-home Children" of Zhiqing in Beijing, Tianjin and Shanghai]. *Zhongguo Qingnian Yanjiu* 中国青年研究 *6*: 31–33.
Hekman, Susan J. 1986. *Hermeneutics and the Sociology of Knowledge*. Cambridge: Polity Press.
Horwitz, Murray and Jacob M. Rabbie. 1982. "Individuality and Membership in the Intergroup System", in *Social Identity and Intergroup Relations*, edited by Henri Tajfel, 241–277. Cambridge: Cambridge University Press.
Hua Ming and Shen Yang 华铭、沈杨, eds. 1998. *Zhongcheng: jinri Laosanjie* 忠诚:今日老三届 [Loyalty: Laosanjie Nowadays]. Shanghai: Lixin kuaiji chubanshe 立信会计出版社.
Hung, Eva P.W. and Chiu Stephen W.K. 2003. "The Lost Generation Life Course Dynamics and Xiagang in China." *Modern China 29(2)*: 204–236.
Huomu 火木. 1992. *Guangrong yu mengxiang–zhongguo zhiqing ershiwunian shi* 光荣与梦想——中国知青25年史 [Honour and Dream: The Twenty Five Years' History of Zhiqing in China]. Chengdu: Chengdu chubanshe 成都出版社.
Ivory, Paul E. and William R. Lavely. 1977. "Rustication, Demographic Change, and Development in Shanghai." *Asian Survey 17(5)*: 440–455.
Jiang Xun 江迅. 1995. "Laosanjie wenhuare saomiao" 老三届文化热扫描 [Scanning the Laosanjie Cultural Upsurge]. *Mingbao yuekan* 明报月刊 *7*: 49–53.
Jin Dalu 金大陆 ed. 1994. *Kunan yu fengliu: Laosanjie ren de daolu* 苦难与风流:老三届人的道路 [Misery and Prominence: Laosanjie's Road]. Shanghai: Shanghai renmin chubanshe 上海人民出版社.
Jin Dalu 金大陆. 1998. *Shiyun yu mingyun: guanyu Laosanjie ren de shengcun yu fazhan* 世运与命运:关于老三届人的生存与发展 [Situation and Destiny: Laosanjie's Lives and Development]. Shanghai: Shanghai renmin chubanshe 上海人民出版社.
Jin Dalu 金大陆, and Jin Guangyao 金光耀, eds. 2009. *Zhongguo zhishi qingnian shangshanxiaxiang yanjiu wenji* 中国知识青年上山下乡研究文集 [Collected Works on Chinese Zhiqing UMDC]. Shanghai: Shanghai shehuikexueyuanchubanshe 上海社会科学院出版社.

Kirk, Jerome and Marc Miller. 1986. *Reliability and Validity in Qualitative Research.* London: Sage.
Klein, H.K. and M.D. Meyers. 1999. "A Set of Principles for Conducting and Evaluating Interpretive Field Studies in Information Systems." *MIS Quarterly 23(1)*: 67–93.
Lewin, Kurt. 1946. "Action Research and Minority Problems." *Journal of Social Issues 2(4)*: 34–46.
Lewin, Kurt. 1951. *Field Theory in Social Science: Selected Theoretical Papers.* Edited by D. Cartwright. New York: Harper & Row.
Li Jianping 李剑萍. 2002a."Ershi shiji zhongguo xuezhi wenti de lishi yanjiu" 20世纪中国学制问题的历史研究 [A Historical Study on the Length of Schooling in China in the Twentieth Century], in *Huadong shifan daxue xuebao (Jiaoyu kexue ban)* 华东师范大学学报(教育科学版)3: 84–89.
Li Junping 李珺平. 2002b. "Fangqi 'Zhiqing qingjie' zouxiang chengming zhi jing – zhongguo wenhua xiaoji jiceng de dangdai ge'an fenxi" 放弃"知青情结"走向澄明之境－－中国文化消极积层的当代个案分析 [Abandon the "Zhiqing Complex" and Move towards Clarity – A Contemporary Case Study on the Negative Layer of Chinese Culture]. *Shehuikexue luntan* 社会科学论坛 4.
Liu Shuang 刘双. 1999. "Choulou de Laosanjie" 丑陋的老三届 [Ugly Laosanjie]. *Huanghe* 黄河 2.
Liu Wenjie 刘文杰. 1998a. "Zhiqing zhengce da tiaozheng jishi" 知青政策大调整纪实 [A Record of Significant Adjustments of Zhiqing Policies]. *Dangshi tiandi* 党史天地 9: 12–17.
Liu Xiaomeng 刘小萌 1994a. "Shangshanxiaxiang zhishi qingnian de hunyin wenti" 上山下乡知识青年的婚姻问题 [Zhiqing's Marriage Problems]. *Qingnian yanjiu* 青年研究 8.
Liu Xiaomeng 刘小萌 1994b. "Xifang xuezhe dui 'Zhiqing shangshanxiaxiang yundong' de yanjiu" 西方学者对"知青上山下乡运动"的研究 [Western Scholars' Research on the "Zhiqing UMDC Movement"]. *Qingnian yanjiu* 青年研究 3: 29–32.
Liu Xiaomeng 刘小萌 1995."'Xuetonglun'yu 'Zhiqing shangshanxiaxiang yundong'" 血统论与知青上山下乡运动 [The Decent Theory and the UMDC Movement]. *Qingnian yanjiu* 青年研究 2: 33–37.
Liu Xiaomeng 刘小萌 1997. "Wenge zhong zai xuetonglun zhongya xia de zhiqing" 文革中在血统论重压下的知青 [Zhiqing Who Were under the Pressure of the Decent Theory during the Cultural Revolution]. *Dangshi chunqiu* 党史春秋 11: 50–54.
Liu Xiaomeng 刘小萌 1998b. *Zhongguo Zhiqing shi: Dachao (1966–1980)* 中国知青史:大潮 (1953–1968) [History of Zhiqing in China: The Spring Tide (1966–1980)]. Beijing: Zhongguo shehui kexue chubanshe 中国社会科学出版社.
Liu Xiaomeng 刘小萌. 2003. *Zhongguo Zhiqing koushushi* 中国知青口述史 [Oral History of Chinese Zhiqing]. Beijing: Zhongguo shehuikexue chubanshe 中国社会科学出版社.
Marshall, Martin N. 1996. "Sampling for Qualitative Research." *Family Practice 13*: 522–525.
Mason, Mark. 2010. "Sample Size and Saturation in PhD Studies Using Qualitative Interviews." *Forum: Qualitative Social Research 11(3)*: 1–19.

References

McLaren, Anne. 1979. "The Educated Youth Return: The Poster Campaign in Shanghai from November 1978 to March 1979." *The Australian Journal of Chinese Affairs* 2: 1–20.

Mi Hedu 米鹤都. 1999. "Xi shangshanxiaxiang yundong de qiyuan" 析上山下乡运动的起源 [Analysing the Origin of the UMDC Movement]. *Dangdai Zhongguoshi yanjiu* 当代中国史研究 2: 95–97.

O'Rand, A.M. 1998. "Observations on the Practice of Life Course Research", in *Methods of Life Course Research: Qualitative and Quantitative Approaches*, edited by Janet Z. Giele and Glen H. Elder, Jr, 52–74. London: Sage.

Patton, Michael Quinn. 2002 [1980]. *Qualitative Research and Evaluation Methods*. Thousand Oaks, CA: Sage.

Peng Xizhe 彭希哲 and Ren Yuan 任远. 1998. "Cong 'Zhiqing yidai' de zhiye liudong kan shehui bianqian" 从"知青一代"的职业流动看社会变迁 [Judging Social Changes from Occupational Mobility of the "Zhiqing Generation"]. *Shehuixue yanjiu* 社会学研究 *1*: 76–83.

Peräkylä, Anssi. 2004. "Reliability and Validity in Research Based on Naturally Occurring Social Interaction", in *Qualitative Research: Theory, Method and Practice*, edited by David Silverman, 365–382. London: Sage.

Piper, W., M. Marrache, R. Lacroix, A. Richardson and B. Jones. 1983. "Cohesion as a Basic Bond in Groups." *Human Relations 36*, 93–108.

Prybyla, Jan S. 1975. "Hsia-Fang: The Economics and Politics of Rustication in China." *Pacific Affairs 48(2)*: 153–172.

Qiu Xinmu 邱新睦. 2001. "Zhishi qingnian shangshanxiaxiang yanjiu zongshu" 知识青年上山下乡研究综述 [A Review of Research on "Zhiqing UMDC"]. *Nanjiazhou zhongguo zhiqing xiehui huikan* 南加州中国知青协会会刊 *3*: 6–13.

Sausmikat, Nora. 1998a. "Female Autobiographies from the Cultural Revolution: Returned Fixing Educated Women in the 1990s", in *Internal and International Migration: Chinese Perspectives*, edited by F. Pieke Richmond, 297–314. Surrey: Carson Press.

Sausmikat, Nora. 1998b. "Resisting Current Stereotypes: Former Rusticated Women between Divergent Personal and Collective Memories and Identities" (paper, The 14th World Congress of Sociology, Montreal, 26 July–1 August 1998).

Scharping, Thomas. 1981. *Umsiedlungsprogramme fur Chinas Jugend 1955–1980: Probleme der Stadt-Land-Beziehungen in der chinesischen Entwicklungspolitik*. Hamburg: Institut fur Asienkunde.

Shi Jing 史镜, Li Mingqi 李明启 and Xing Baoyu 邢宝玉. 1986. "Fu Neimenggu Shangshanxiaxiang zhishi qingnian de lishi yu xianzhuang diaocha" 赴内蒙古上山下乡知识青年的历史与现状调查 [A Survey on the History and the Status Quo of Zhiqing Who Went to the Inner Mongolia]. *Shehuixue yanjiu* 社会学研究 *6*: 36–43.

Silverman, David. 2001. *Interpreting Qualitative Data: Methods for Analysing Talk, Text and Interaction*. London: Sage.

Stanley, Rosen. 1981. *The Role of Sent-down Youth in the Chinese Cultural Revolution: The Case of Guangzhou*. Berkeley, CA: University of California Press.

Stryker, Sheldon and Peter J. Burke. 2000. "The Past, Present and Future of an Identity Theory." *Social Psychology Quarterly 63(4)*: 284–297.

Tajfel, Henri. 1969. "Cognitive Aspects of Prejudice." *Journal of Social Issues 25*: 79–97.
Tajfel, Henri. 1970. "Experiments in Intergroup Discrimination." *Scientific American 223*: 96–102.
Tajfel, Henri. 1974. "Social Identity and Intergroup Behaviour." *Social Science Information 13*: 65–93.
Tajfel, Henri. 1981. *Human Groups and Social Categories*. Cambridge: Cambridge University Press.
Tajfel, Henri, ed. 1982. *Social Identity and Intergroup Relations*. Cambridge: Cambridge University Press.
Tuckett, A.G. 2004, "Truth Telling in Clinical Practice and the Arguments For and Against: A Review of the Literature." *Nursing Ethics 11(5)*: 500–513.
Turner, John C. 1982. "Towards a Cognitive Definition of the Social Group", in *Social Identity and Intergroup Relations*, edited by Henri Tajfel, 15–40. Cambridge: Cambridge University Press.
Turner, John C., Michael A. Hogg, Penelope J. Oakes, Stephen D. Reicher and Margaret S. Wetherell. 1987. *Rediscovering the Social Group: A Self-Categorization Theory*. Cambridge, MA: Basil Blackwell.
Unger, Jonathan. 1979. "China's Troubled Down-to-the-Countryside Campaign." *Contemporary China 2*: 79–92.
Van Manen, Max. 1990. *Researching Lived Experience: Human Science for an Action Sensitive Pedagogy*. New York: State University of New York Press.
Wang Jiang 王江, ed. 1995. *Jiehou huihuang: zai monan zhong jueqi de Zhiqing Laosanjie, gongheguo disandai ren* 劫后辉煌:在磨难中崛起的知青老三届,共和国第三代人 [Glory after Suffering: Laosanjie Emerged from a Long Trial, the Third Generation of the Republic]. Beijing: Guangming ribao chubanshe 光明日报社出版社.
Wang Jiang 王江. 1996. "Guanyu 'Laosanjie' ren yanjiu de fangfalun" 关于"老三届"人研究的方法论 [On the Methodology of Laosanjie Studies]. *Zhongguo qingnian yanjiu* 中国青年研究 *4*: 13–15.
Wang Xiaobo 王小波. 1995. "Yi pingchangxin kan 'Laosanjie'" 以平常心看"老三届" [Viewing the "Laosanjie" Soberly]. *Zhongguo qingnian yanjiu* 中国青年研究 *6*: 26–27.
White, D. Gordon. 1974. "The Politics of Hsia-hsiang Youth." *The China Quarterly 59*: 491–517.
Whyte, Martin King. 1975. "Inequality and Stratification in China." *The China Quarterly 64*: 684–711.
Willis, Jerry W. 2007. *Foundations of Qualitative Research*. Thousand Oaks, CA: Sage.
Wu Liping 吴丽萍. 1997. "Jiating chushen yu zhishiqingnian shangshan xiaxiang" 家庭出身与知识青年上山下乡 [Family Origins and the UMDC]. *Zhongguo qingnian yanjiu* 中国青年研究 *5*: 34–35.
Wu Siyuan 邬思源. 1996. "Zhishi qingnian shangshanxiaxiang yundong yanjiu zongshu" 知识青年上山下乡运动研究综述 [A Review of Research on Zhiqing UMDC Movement]. *Dangshi wenhui* 党史文汇 *9*: 31–33.

Xiaojian 晓剑 and Guo Xiaodong 郭小东. 1999. *Laosanjie: yu gongheguo tongxin* 老三届:与共和国同行 [Laosanjie: Walk Along with the Republic]. Beijing: Zhongguo wenlian chuban gongsi 中国文联出版公司.

Xu Youyu 徐友渔. 1998. "Zhiqing jingli he xiaxiang yundong – geti jingyan yu jiti yishi de duihua" 知青经历和下乡运动 – – 个体经验与集体意识的对话 [Zhiqing Experiences and the UMDC Movement: A Conversation between Individual Experience and Collective Consciousness]. *Beijing wenxue* 北京文学 6: 29–32.

Yang Bin. 2009. "'We Want to Go Home!' The Great Petition of the Zhiqing, Xishuangbanna, Yunnan, 1978–1979." *The China Quarterly 198*: 401–421.

Yang Fan 杨帆. 1995. "Diwuzhong fenhua: daiji fenhua" 第五种分化:代际分化 [The Fifth Kind of Differentiation: Intergenerational Differentiation]. *Zhongguo qingnian yanjiu* 中国青年研究 6: 27–28.

Yang, Guobin. 2003. "China's Zhiqing Generation: Nostalgia, Identity, and Cultural Resistance in the 1990s." *Modern China 29(3)*: 267–296.

Yang, Guobin. 2005. "Days of Old Are Not Puffs of Smoke: Three Hypotheses on Collective Memories of the Cultural Revolution." *The China Review 5(2)*: 13–41.

Zhang Hua 张化. 1987. "Shilun 'wenhua dageming' zhong de zhishi qingnian shangshanxiaxiang yundong" 试论"文化大革命"中的知识青年上山下乡运动 [A Tentative Study on the Zhishi Qingnian UMDC Movement during the "Cultural Revolution"]. *Dangshi ziliao tongxun* 党史资料通讯 4: 9–16.

Zhang Shu 张曙. 2001. "'Wenge' zhong de zhishi qingnian shangshanxiaxiang yundong yanjiu shuping" "文革"中的知识青年上山下乡运动研究述评 [A Review of Research on Zhiqing UMDC Movement during the "Cultural Revolution"]. *Dangdai zhongguoshi yanjiu* 当代中国史研究 2.

Zhao Wenyuan 赵文远. 2009. "Shangshan xiaxiang zhishi qingnian hukou qianyi wenti yanjiu" 上山下乡知识青年户口迁移问题研究 [A Study on the Issue of Zhiqing's Household Residence Transfer], in *Zhongguo zhishiqingnian shangshanxiaxiang yanjiu wenji* 中国知识青年上山下乡研究文集 [Collected Works on UMDC Studies], edited by Jin Dalu and Jin Guangyao, 500–508. Shanghai: Shanghai Academy of Social Sciences Press.

Zhou Xueguang and Hou Liren. 1999. "Children of the Cultural Revolution: The State and the Life Course in the People's Republic of China." *American Sociological Review 64(1)*: 12–36.

Zhou Xueguang, Nancy Brandon Tuma and Phyllis Moen. 1996. "Stratification Dynamics under State Socialism: The Case of Urban China, 1949–1993." *Social Forces 74(3)*: 759–796.

Zhu Xueqin 朱学勤. 1995. "Sixiangshi shang de shizongzhe" 思想史上的失踪者 [Missing People in Intellectual History]. *Dushu* 读书 *10*: 55–63.

Index

2/12 Instruction 22
12/22 Instruction 19, 22, 30

activist protests 23–4, 60
affective outcomes in group formation 50, 52–4, 71–2, 77, 83
age of going to countryside 15, 27, 28
agricultural cooperatives 13
alienation, feelings of 46–7, 54, 62
attraction-based group cohesion 54, 55

Beijing Youth Voluntary Reclamation Team 13
belonging, feelings of 50, 54
Bernstein, Thomas P. 24
birth years 26, 27, 28
blending in periods: into countryside 44–8; back into urban society 67–71
Bonnin, Michel 83 n.2, 83 n.3
bourgeoisie 14, 16, 19
broadening of the mind 69–70, 76
brotherhood/sisterhood 53
Brown, Rupert 9, 10, 63

Cai Lijian 17
category distinctions 6–9, 45–6, 55, 68, 77, 80–1
Cheng Zihua 23
child-bearing 33, 78–9
Chinese New Year 51, 55
Climax of Socialism in Rural China, The 13

cluster effects 74
cognitive processes 4–8, 50, 59, 63, 67–8, 78
cohesiveness of the group: attraction-based group cohesion 54, 55; commitment-based cohesion 53–4, 55, 73; configuration processes 50, 53; post-Zhiqing era 72–3, 82–3
cohorts 25–9, 86
collective activities, Zhiqing themed 71–4, 77, 78, 86
collective farms 43
collective households 48–9, 54
collective identities 2
collective life 48–52
commitment-based cohesion 53–4, 55, 73
communes 21
Communist Youth League 16
compulsory activities 49–50
conflicts and problems 22, 24, 47, 52, 54
conscription 61
construction corps 43
constructionist perspectives 4
contextual shift 7, 52, 71, 87
coping strategies 11, 58, 69–71, 87
corps, collective life in 48–9
costs: of trips back home 55–6; of UMDC 22, 24
cultural heritage 73
Cultural Revolution 17, 26, 27, 28, 29–30, 31–2

Index

Decision on mobilizing and organizing urban Zhiqing to participate in socialist construction in the countryside (draft) 16
degree of identification 10–11
demonstrations 60 *see also* protests
Deng Xiaoping 23, 34
depersonalization 6–7, 10, 45, 55, 68
deskilling 22
developmental trajectory 25, 26, 85, 86
dialectical approach 85, 87
diligence 69, 80
Ding Yizhuang 1, 12 n.1, 13, 14, 16, 33, 36 n.4, 36 n.5
disabled people 20, 22, 24
discrimination 62, 65, 67–71, 78, 86
Displacement System 38 n.35
distancing from the group 71
domicile control 17 *see also* household registration system
downsizing of the project 23–4 *see also* termination of the Zhiqing project
duration of stay in the countryside 27, 28

education: completion or otherwise of secondary 27; compulsory study of political documents 49–50; effects of limited education 32, 34, 40–2, 62–3, 64; life course approach 31–2; self-teaching 40–2
Elder, Glen H. 13, 25, 26, 88
embarrassment 57–8
emergency measures 23–4
emotional ties 50, 53, 71–2, 77, 83
employment: career success attributed to UMDC experiences 65–6; expansion of urban employment 23, 24; filling parents' job positions 61; job recruitment policies 27; mass layoffs 32, 34, 63, 64; pressure caused by abrupt termination of UMDC 62, 64; unemployment 13, 14, 24, 33, 62, 64
equalitarian ideology 2

evening schools 41
extreme groups 46

family backgrounds 33–4, 64
family-like nature of collective households 54–5
family separation/breakdown 62, 75
farms, Zhiqing 23, 43, 48–9
farm work 19, 44–6
food 47, 52, 55–7
fraud 20
friendships 44–5, 53, 54–5, 71–2
fun activities 50–1
future research 87–8

Gang of Four 22
generation gap 81
Giele, Janet Z. 25
gratitude, feelings of 47, 66, 70
Great Leap Forward 14–15
grey zone between rural and urban 46, 48, 58, 65, 87
group cohesiveness: attraction-based group cohesion 54, 55; commitment-based cohesion 53–4, 55, 73; configuration processes 50, 53; post-Zhiqing era 72–3, 82–3
group-identity configuration processes: conclusions on 85, 86; in the countryside 39–59; group-individual continuum 5; integrated group-identity configuration 8–11; post-Zhiqing era 60–84
group-individual continuum 2, 5–6
"group-mode" self-concept 5
group solidarity 10, 71, 72, 73
guardians 22
Gu Hongzhang 15, 21

happiness 51
hard work ethos 45, 47, 66, 69
helplessness 57, 64
higher education reform 17, 23, 31
historical context 13–38

98 Index

holidays/home visits (back to the city) 55–8
homogenization 10
hopelessness 43, 57
Horwitz, Murray 50, 53, 72
household registration system 17, 62
households, collective 48–9, 54
Houwujie (Post-Five Grade): as cohort 23, 25, 26, 28–9; and the Cultural Revolution 30; education 32; ideologies 30; and the Reform and Open era 31; structural lag 33
Huining County 18
Huixiang Zhiqing 12 n.2, 14, 36 n.2
human resources 33–4, 64–5
humiliation and shame 57–8

identity: definition 85; group membership configured in time 3–11; identity loss 2; life course approach 25–35; Zhiqing identity 1–3 *see also* social identity theory
identity theory 88 *see also* social identity theory
ideologies 14, 16, 18, 30, 35, 47
illness certifications 61
individual-group continuum 2, 5–6
"individual-mode" self-concept 5
inferiority complex 56
ingroup committment 53, 54
ingroup favouritism 78, 80–1
ingroup-outgroup meta-contrast 6, 43–4, 46–7, 48, 65, 75
instrumental outcomes in group formation 50, 53
interdependencies among individuals 50, 72
interdependencies of fate 50
intergenerational effects 78–81
intergroup differentiation 5–6, 11, 46, 63, 78, 80–1
intergroup discrimination 68, 78
intergroup engagement 87
interpersonal relationships 11, 53, 68, 74–81

inter-provincial networks 54
interrelated lives 34–5, 52–5

Jinghong Farm 23
job recruitment policies, relaxation of 27

kinship-like relationships 53

labouring work 14, 16–18, 22, 44–6, 52, 63
Laochuyi 26, 32
Laogaosan 26–7, 32
Laosanjie: as cohort 19, 25, 26–7; and the Cultural Revolution 29, 30–1; education 32; idealist characteristics 30; structural lag 28, 33
latent effects 46, 86
leadership/management 49, 51, 66
Leading Cadre System 21, 22
Leading Group Office of Zhiqing UMDC 15
Leading Group of Resettlement Work of Agriculture and Forestry Office 15
leftist ideologies 16, 18, 19, 22
length of stay in the countryside 27, 28
life chances 31–4
life course approach 13, 25–35, 87, 88
life cycle theory 25
life span theory 25
life stories as units of analysis 39–40
Li Qinglin 20
Liu Xiaomeng 12 n.3, 19, 22, 74
longitudinal approach 85, 88
lost generation 1, 3, 79, 86

management/leadership 49, 51, 66
manual labour 14, 16–18, 22, 44–6, 52, 63
Mao Zedong 13, 19, 20, 22, 30, 60
marriage 33, 53, 62, 68, 74–8
Massive Retreat 60–1, 75
mass layoffs 32, 34, 63, 64
meaning, and the analytical approach 39–40

Minutes of the National Conference on the UMDC Work 22–3
money 55–7
morale of the group 20, 22
motivational explanation 5–6, 8, 11, 48, 63, 80
movie watching 51

narrative analysis 88
National Conference on Labour Employment Work 24
National Day 51
National Planning Conference 20–1
nepotism 33
normative behaviours 45, 50, 86–7
norms and prototypes 7–10, 50, 58, 68
Notification of Resuming Revolution in Classes 31
Notification of University Entrance Examination Reform 17

only children 20, 22
O'Rand, Angela 25
outgroup-ingroup meta-contrast 6, 43–4, 46–7, 48, 65, 75
Outline of National Agricultural Development from 1956 to 1967 (draft) 14

parent-child relationships 78–81
peasants: transformation into 44–8; Zhiqing-peasant differentiation 45; Zhiqing-peasant marriage 75; Zhiqing-peasant relationships 46–8, 75, 82–3
permanency, intentions of UMDC 44
permanent urban residency 62, 64, 75
personality, benefits of Zhiqing for 69–70, 76–7
personality expository model of identity 4
personal relationships 11, 52–5, 68, 74–81
phase, period in countryside as temporary 22, 30

political activism 18, 19
Political Bureau 14
political movement, UMDC as 16
positive outcomes 47–8, 69–70, 80–1
post-Zhiqing era 24, 54, 60–84, 86
poverty 19 *see also* socio-economic disadvantage
power relationships, changing 48
preferential policies 23
prejudice 42, 63, 67–9
problems and conflicts 22, 24, 47, 52, 54
processes, social groups as 4
production teams: better conditions in 43; collective life 48–9; relocation from 23; resettlement to 15, 17, 20–1, 23–4
Prosper Zhiqing Culture 73
protests 23–4, 60, 62
prototyping: and depersonalization 55; and discrimination 68; group cohesiveness 48, 54, 58; internalization 10; norms and prototypes 7–10, 50, 58, 67; positive prototypes 66; in the re-settling phase 65; RII mechanism 45–6; solidification of conventions/norms 45–6, 48, 50
psychological implications 3–10, 19, 45, 71, 74, 78

quasi-kinship 53
Qu Zhe 17

Rabbie, Jacob M. 50, 53, 72
reading, for self-study 41
recreational activities 50–1
red guards 17, 27, 30
re-education theory 18–19, 22, 30, 47
Referent Information Influence (RII) 8, 9–10, 45–6, 50
Reform and Open policy: and the cohorts 28, 30, 31; economic transformation 34, 71; education 32; generation gap, intensified 81;

socio-cultural transformation 2;
socio-economic status, changes in 34
registered permanent residency 16–17
regulations 49–50
relationships: friendships 44–5, 53, 54–5, 71–2; interrelated lives 34–5; marriage 33, 53, 62, 68, 74–8; parent-child relationships 78–81; personal relationships 11, 52–5, 68, 74–81; as source of employment 64
relative deprivation 58, 70–1
rent-seeking behaviour 20
Reporting Conference of Resettling Urban Redundant Staff and Young Students in State Farms, Forest Farms, Pastures and Fisheries 15
Report on Organizing Urban Zhiqing to Engage in Socialist Construction in the Countryside 16
Report on Recruitment (pilot) of Beijing University and Qinghua University 20
research into Zhiqing 22, 73, 87–8
resettlement: back to city 60–2; destinations 15, 17, 20–1, 23–4; fees 16, 19
Resettlement Office 15
retirement 27–8, 37 n.26, 71, 72–3
returning to the city: blending in period 67–71; collective life 51–2; Massive Retreat 60–2; painful emotions 56–7; structural lag 33; termination of the Zhiqing project 23–4, 60–84; various channels for 22; visits home (to the city) 55–8
returning to the countryside (for visits) 81–3
reverse side of identification 10–11
Review and Summary of Zhiqing Work over 25 Years 24
revolutionary aspirations 18, 22
rights and obligations 16
RII (Referent Information Influence) 8, 9–10, 45–6, 50
rules and regulations 50
rural society, blending into 44–8

rural-urban gap 19, 46, 56, 62, 75
Rusticated Youth 1

sadness, feelings of 43
schooling *see* education
secondary education, completion or otherwise of 27
second home 82–3
Second National Conference 22–3, 60
self-concept 5–8, 68–9
self-identification 43
self-teaching 40–2
Sent-down Youth 1
settling-in phases: comparison of the two 65–6; in countryside 42–4, 45; post-Zhiqing era 64–7
shame and humiliation 57–8
Shanghai Youth Voluntary Reclamation Team 13
Shangshan xiaxiang yundong *see* UMDC
sisterhood/brotherhood 53
six-year plan 21
skills 22, 34, 65–6, 80
slogans 22, 30
social categorization 8–9, 10, 46, 65, 68
social cognition 63
social comparison 7–8, 10, 50
social groups as processes 4–8
social identification 10
social identity theory: alternatives to 88; and collective Zhiqing activities 71; definition 3–11; in future work 87; and Zhiqing group identity 39, 43, 63, 70–1, 85
socialism 27, 28
socially-determined cognitive construction 4–8
social networks, widening of 34–5 *see also* relationships
social-psychological perspective 3–11, 86, 87
social status, inferior 19 *see also* discrimination
social stratification 54
socio-economic disadvantage: conclusions on 86; and education

42; life course approach 34; and marriage 76; perceived as generational issue 79; post-Zhiqing era 62, 63, 64, 67, 74; socio-historical context 13–14, 17
socio-historical context 13–38, 79, 81, 85, 88
socio-political powers 16
solidarity, group 10, 71, 72, 73
special occasions 51
spiritual support 73
State Labour Bureau 24
statistics: marriage 84 n.8; Massive Retreat 61; returners 24; UMDC (Up to the Mountains Down to the Countryside Movement) 1, 17–19, 27, 28
stereotyping: depersonalization 10; and discrimination 69; education level 42, 63; Zhiqing identity 42, 45–6; Zhiqing-peasant marriage 75
strikes (protest movements) 23–4, 60
structural lag 28, 33, 62, 74, 78, 80
Stryker, Sheldon 88
subgroups 25–9, 54, 74
substitution policy 62
supervision 49

Tajfel, Henri 3–6, 8, 9, 53, 68, 78
Tajfel's Law 5, 6, 11, 46, 63
"taking root" 22
task interdependence 45, 50
temporary, period in countryside as 22, 30
termination of the Zhiqing project 23–4, 60–84, 86
thematic analysis 39–40
Trial Provisions about Several Issues of 'UMDC' by the State Council 22–3
trustworthy/untrustworthy family backgrounds 33
Turner, John C. 4, 6, 8, 9, 11, 48, 53, 63, 80

ultra-left ideologies 16, 22, 42
UMDC (Up to the Mountains Down to the Countryside Movement): end of 23–4, 60–84, 86; history 1, 13–24; history of the name 14; and the life course approach 29, 30; and unemployment 33
unemployment 13, 14, 24, 33, 62, 64
university: and the Massive Retreat 61; self-study for 40–2; University/College Entrance Examination 17, 23, 31–2, 63; worker-peasant-soldier students 31, 41, 61, 63
urban-rural gap 19, 46, 56, 62, 75
urban worker-Zhiqing marriage 75–6

Van Manen, Max 39
visits back to the countryside 81–3
visits home (to the city) 55–8
voluntary movements 17–18

Wang Zhen 23
worker-peasant-soldier students 31, 41, 61, 63
work unit responsibility 62
Wu Guixian 37 n.18

Xinwujie (The New Five Grades): as cohort 21, 25, 26; and the Cultural Revolution 30; education 32; ideologies 30; structural lag 33

youth reclamation teams 13
Yunnan Zhiqing protests 23–4, 60

Zhao Wenyuan 36 n.9, 75–6
Zhiqing, definition 1
Zhiqing complex 3, 72
Zhiqing cultural upsurge 71–4
Zhisi qingnian 1
Zhou Enlai 15
Zhuzhou model 21–2, 27–8

eBooks
from Taylor & Francis

Helping you to choose the right eBooks for your Library

Add to your library's digital collection today with Taylor & Francis eBooks. We have over 50,000 eBooks in the Humanities, Social Sciences, Behavioural Sciences, Built Environment and Law, from leading imprints, including Routledge, Focal Press and Psychology Press.

Choose from a range of subject packages or create your own!

Benefits for you
- Free MARC records
- COUNTER-compliant usage statistics
- Flexible purchase and pricing options
- All titles DRM-free.

Benefits for your user
- Off-site, anytime access via Athens or referring URL
- Print or copy pages or chapters
- Full content search
- Bookmark, highlight and annotate text
- Access to thousands of pages of quality research at the click of a button.

Free Trials Available
We offer free trials to qualifying academic, corporate and government customers.

eCollections

Choose from over 30 subject eCollections, including:

Archaeology	Language Learning
Architecture	Law
Asian Studies	Literature
Business & Management	Media & Communication
Classical Studies	Middle East Studies
Construction	Music
Creative & Media Arts	Philosophy
Criminology & Criminal Justice	Planning
Economics	Politics
Education	Psychology & Mental Health
Energy	Religion
Engineering	Security
English Language & Linguistics	Social Work
Environment & Sustainability	Sociology
Geography	Sport
Health Studies	Theatre & Performance
History	Tourism, Hospitality & Events

For more information, pricing enquiries or to order a free trial, please contact your local sales team:
www.tandfebooks.com/page/sales

www.tandfebooks.com

For Product Safety Concerns and Information please contact our EU representative GPSR@taylorandfrancis.com
Taylor & Francis Verlag GmbH, Kaufingerstraße 24, 80331 München, Germany

www.ingramcontent.com/pod-product-compliance
Lightning Source LLC
Chambersburg PA
CBHW070542300426
44113CB00011B/1758